THE
TRIM
COURSE

Published by Aardvark Business Management

ISBN: 978-0-9928954-0-2

Printed by Bell and Bain Limited, Glasgow

This book is dedicated to you, the reader. I hope that it makes a real difference to your life, making you a happier and more contented person and helping you make the world a better place.

Life is for living.
Do it the best way you can!
ANON

ACKNOWLEDGEMENTS

Many people have helped me along the way – first in developing The **TRIM** Course, and then in turning it into this book. I would particularly like to thank the people below – there are too many of you to list, so if you don't find your name here please don't think it is because I have forgotten you!

Jack Galbraith, my Housemaster, who got me the Head Boy's job in 1974. That forced me to up my game!

My bosses at Benton & Bowles – Alan, Richard, Sue, Carol and Tony, who all threw so many balls and plates at me that without **TRIM** to help me I would have failed completely in my first job!

Nigel Stubley, my Deputy Managing Director at The Pasty Company, for being the first **TRIM** trainee: "We might have our disagreements, Stuart, but you always do as you say you will and remember everything! Please teach me!"

Theresa Houston, Chief Executive of "Scotland the Brand", my first delegate at a **TRIM** Course, who commented "This is really great. You will have to teach everyone!"

John McAndrew of Scottish Enterprise, who early in my running of The **TRIM** Courses said "You really should write the book".

My wife Shona and children Sandy & Jeannie, who have encouraged me to develop **TRIM** with them as part of our family.

John Brand for ghost writing, and helping me at every stage of the **TRIM** book. My sister Sheena said to me "As I read the book, I can see you talking to me."

Janey Boyd for all of her wonderful creative visuals that are such an integral part of the book, and, like John, helping me at every stage.

And, last but not least, to everyone across the world who has been on a **TRIM** Course, helped me develop the **TRIM** ideas and given me great advice in putting the book together.

Needless to say, all errors and omissions in the book are mine alone!

My thanks to you all.

Stuart Richardson
EDINBURGH, APRIL 2014

Contents

Introduction

> I'm a guy who can't function well in life...
>
> WOODY ALLEN

WELL DONE!

Congratulations! You have started on a journey that will help you to make your own life more satisfying, and improve the lives of other people you deal with.

By picking up this book, and reading this introduction, you have shown that you know you can change your life – and you're prepared to find out how.

Read on!

TRIM's easy-to-use tools and techniques will make you better organised, more productive, happier and more popular. They are not designed for 'business people' or 'self-improvers'. They are, quite simply, for human beings – whether in the business environment or at home dealing with family and friends.

TRIM is a personal programme – it's all about you, and how to improve your life. You might think this sounds pretty self-centred, even selfish. But as you will discover, once you're in control of your own life, you will also be able to contribute far more effectively to the lives of the people you live and work with. Be happy – and make the world a better place!

By showing you how to make your life more fulfilling, **TRIM** increases your efficiency and effectiveness – and makes life more fun. It's about making the most of the opportunities you have every day, managing information and relationships, and using time effectively.

Above all, **TRIM** is about putting you back in control of your life. Of course you can't always do what you want. But you can make sure that you use your own resources – your time and your abilities – in the way that best suits your own aims and ambitions. Best of all, as you gain control of your own life, your family, friends and people you work with will value you more. You won't make promises you can't deliver, or miss a meeting you forgot to put in your diary. As you gain a reputation for being reliable and helpful you will be trusted and people will seek your advice – and you will be helping to improve not just your own life, but the lives of others too.

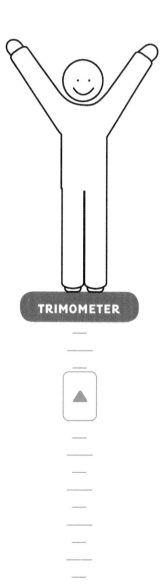

TRIMOMETER

WHY DO YOU NEED TRIM?

How many people do you know who are completely happy with their lives? Probably "damn few, and they're all dead" as the old Scots saying goes. Almost everyone would like to 'do life better'. Very few of us feel that we are living life to the full. We're all frustrated by the things that we know we're not doing as well as we could, the arrangements that are going wrong, the commitments which maybe we shouldn't have made....the list goes on!

Everyone has too much to do – at work, at home, just carrying on the business of living.

We always seem to be rushing around.
We keep forgetting to do things.
We let people down.
We let ourselves down.

There never seems to be enough time to get everything done.

It just seems to get worse and worse –
We're involved with more and more people and organisations.

We're exposed to more and more information.

We need to manage people and situations more effectively.

And the pressures are growing...

You don't need me to tell you that losing control of your life is stressful. When you're trying to catch up with your commitments – rushing to get to a meeting you're already late for, desperately searching for the birthday present you should have bought a week ago – your heartrate goes up, your muscles tense, and you're liable to start making silly mistakes. If you stay like this for long periods it can make you ill. It certainly affects your ability to get things done!

When you know that you are in command, you will be more relaxed, more confident, better focused – you will simply 'feel better about yourself'.

Because being in control makes you more calm, you will have become generally easier to deal with and better to know. Everyone has had the annoyance of being let down when someone doesn't turn up for a meeting, or fails to do what they said they would. If you can show that you are not that kind of person, that you can be trusted to deliver, that you get things done coolly and without pointless arguing or being confrontational, people will like you and will enjoy working – or just being – with you. In this book you will learn how to manage other people's expectations – and then exceed them.

WHO BENEFITS?

TRIM will help anyone who wants to achieve their goals in life.

It doesn't matter where you sit within an organisation, whether it's the Ford Motor Company or simply your family. The higher up you are, the bigger the stick you can wave and the more carrots you have to give away. If you're lower down the tree you probably have less direct power to influence the way things happen. But in every case, to make things work the way you want them to work, you will need to be more efficient and more effective. **TRIM** will help you.

Everyone – really, everyone! – has to make compromises, negotiate how they are going to get things done and when they will have to deliver on their promises. Of course you can't always end up with exactly the result you want, but **TRIM's** techniques let you make sure that you achieve the best possible outcome for yourself.

Of course before you can start to achieve your goals, you need to have a pretty clear idea of what they are! In Chapter 3 we will look at how you can set realistic but achievable goals – and how you will know that you are attaining them.

GOAL ONE?

GOAL TWO?

GOAL THREE?

WHAT SKILLS WILL YOU DEVELOP?

As well as the ability to weigh up the costs and benefits of your actions, you'll learn to use **TRIM's** unique tools and techniques to keep control of the information that bombards you, and to manage the constant demands on your time. If you practice the lessons in the book, you will never again forget a meeting or make a promise that you can't deliver. And that's a promise from me!

TRIM will teach you how to store and process your 'information blizzard' – from meetings, phone calls and even casual encounters in the street. How often have you thought "I must remember that..." and then completely forgotten it? No more!

We've all found ourselves taking on so many commitments that we just can't cope – and then another urgent requirement comes along, and something just has to give. **TRIM** will show you how to arrange your diary so that you stay in control – and when things do go wrong, how to prevent a minor hiccup from turning into a major embarrassment.

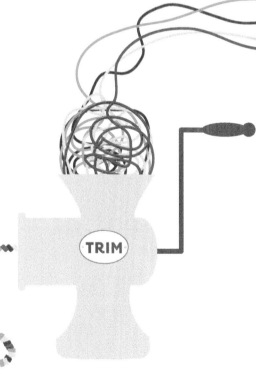

prepared

organised

in control

WHO DO I THINK YOU ARE?

By reading this book, you are already demonstrating that you
would like to be in command of your own life – that you want to
make the decisions, rather than always taking the orders. Here
are a few of the assumptions I'm making about you:

YOU MAY BE VERY GOOD AT YOUR JOB
...or at being a Mum or carer – but
you are willing to accept that you
can always do better

YOU ARE AMBITIOUS
You may or may not want to get to
the top of whatever greasy pole you
find yourself on – but you certainly
want to achieve the goals you set for
yourself.

YOU ARE PREPARED TO BE PERSUASIVE
TRIM will teach you how to 'sell' to
others the outcomes that you want
from every situation. That is how you
are going to achieve your goals.

YOU ARE 'SELF-EMPLOYED'
– in other words, you are the only
person who is dedicated to achieving
your goals. Not your boss. Not your
partner. Not your family, or your
friends. Only you.

YOU DO CARE ABOUT BEING VALUED AND LOVED BY THE OTHER PEOPLE IN YOUR LIFE
Within all of your relationships,
across work, outside interests and
your family, you will be most valued
when you deliver as you promised.

YOU WANT TO BE COMFORTABLE IN YOUR RELATIONSHIPS WITH OTHERS
– and at peace with yourself.

Finally, and most important of all –

YOU WANT TO BE HAPPY!

WHO WILL YOU BE WHEN YOU FINISH THE BOOK?

Think of the people you know or work with. Some of them probably have a reputation for being quietly dependable, unflappable and cheery – for getting things done without fuss or fanfare. Others – and I'll bet there are many more of them – are always in a hurry, constantly apologising for being late, often unprepared and likely to bite your head off if you ask them to do something. Which one do you prefer to spend time with? Which one could you rely on to help you sort out a problem?

TRIM is designed to make you the person that other people warm to and want to know! If you use the **TRIM** tools and put the techniques into practice, you can't fail to be reliable and trustworthy. Even better, because you will also be quite sure that what you are doing at any given moment is the best thing to help you attain your own goals, you will be a more contented person.

Of course, if all you do is just read the book, nothing will change! Although I will introduce you to the tools and techniques that will help you to stay in control of your life and your relationships, they can't be 'one size fits all' and it will take a little while for you to adapt **TRIM** to fit your own personal needs. Some of **TRIM's** principles might appear a little strange at first: but if they just came naturally, everyone would be using them already! Persevere! Very soon you will see **TRIM** making a real difference to the way you plan and organise your activities. As you see how some small changes can help you, it will become easier to incorporate the other elements of **TRIM** into your life. Soon it will all become second nature for you.

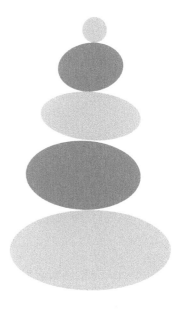

A NOTE ABOUT THE TRIM TOOLS AND TECHNIQUES

Throughout this book I will be talking a lot about 'records' – diaries, notes, folders and so on. Don't be alarmed! Although **TRIM** started life as a paper-based system – and in fact I still like to use real touchy-feely paper for some parts of it – almost all of the **TRIM** tools and techniques transfer very well onto electronic media. Programs and 'software suites' like Microsoft Office, Google Docs and OpenOffice, as well as many apps available for smartphones and tablet computers, contain elements which can be integrated into **TRIM** and work very well to provide the information storage and cross-referencing you'll use. Chapter 10 looks specifically at 'Digital **TRIM**', and throughout the book I will refer to aspects which can be specially well handled electronically.

Nevertheless, it is still clearer and easier to understand the principles of **TRIM** by introducing them as separate elements using plain old paper. As we go along, you will see how these individual bits fit together, and you may well think of your own ways of incorporating them into computer-based programs you are already using.

THE ORIGINS OF TRIM

SEPTEMBER 1974

TRIM originated as long ago as September 1974 – on a Monday morning, my first day as Head Boy of Dollar Academy, a leading Scottish public school. Picture the scene! Morning Assembly has just finished. All the teachers are filing out of the Hall, where I am now on my way to my first class of the 6th Year, my final year after eight years at the school.

Out of the blue, a teacher comes up and asks me to arrange for a prefect to cover his maths class at 11am as he has an emergency dental appointment. "Certainly. No trouble, Mr Jones."

Mr Jones has no sooner moved on when Mrs Glendinning arrives. "Stuart, could you please come and see me sometime today to discuss involving 6th Year pupils in an art project I want to run this term?" "Certainly, Mrs Glendinning – no trouble at all."

Off to my first class of the day? Not yet! One more request! Mr Henderson: "Could you please arrange for three prefects to accompany my Form One biology field trip this afternoon?" "Certainly. No trouble at all, Mr Henderson."

9.05am. My first day as Head Boy. Three time-consuming tasks committed to already, and five minutes late for my first class! If things were going to go on like this through the year, something was going to have to change!

How was I to cope? How was I going to remember everything I had agreed to do? How could I get all these extra duties done without wrecking my own academic work, school days and personal life?

The problem was that, like most people, given the chance I liked nothing better than to relax, doing my own thing all the time – with no responsibilities, except to myself to do whatever I wanted to do, whenever and wherever! Bliss...!

Unfortunately, even at school I had learned that this approach to life just wouldn't work. No pain, no gain! Perhaps I could get by, simply doing the absolute minimum possible to keep people satisfied and let me get on with my own life?

Then the problem really kicked in! I wanted very much to be a great Head Boy, and part of that meant never letting people down. Anyway, I hate letting people down! I hate letting myself down! In my heart of hearts I knew that doing the minimum was never going to be good enough – I had to do my best.

I knew that I had to ensure that every commitment made would be delivered to the very best of my ability. If I agreed to do something, then I would have to make sure that it was done – on time and properly!

So here was the conflict – and I'll be surprised if you haven't faced it too. How can you have enough space to do your own thing, and yet not let yourself or anyone else down? Is it possible to balance these opposing drivers in our mental make-up?

The solution then was exactly the same as it is today. Go back to basics. What did I want out of life? What were my real goals? Whether I liked it or not, my two most central needs – to make people happy and to do my best in everything I do – won the day. It seemed that finding time for my personal priorities would have to wait.

BUT NOW THE GOOD NEWS!

As I began to put together and use the tools and techniques which now underpin the **TRIM** system, it gradually dawned on me that so long as I was in control of what was going on around me, I could 'earn' the ability to spend time on myself. Providing I was on top of all of the commitments I had made (or that had been made for me), I could schedule in 'self time' without any feelings of guilt. Even better, if I was on top of what was coming up in the days ahead of me, I could take control – to some extent at least! – of what I would take on. Providing that I was the one who decided when I would deliver, I was in charge and I could allocate my time to suit myself.

The best thing of all was that I soon learned that 'self time' recharged my batteries. It actually made me better at 'making people happy' – and better able to make sure that I did everything to the best of my ability. My 'self time' was helping me achieve the goals that I myself had set.

So not only did preserving time for myself protect me from 'burning out', it also made me better at reaching my objectives. My conundrum was solved.

Since leaving school all those years ago, I have continued to develop and improve these early techniques and tools through a career as a businessman, successful entrepreneur and business mentor for new companies. Friends and clients asked me to share the secrets with them, and so I developed **TRIM** into a coherent system which worked not only in the business world but more generally, for people who just want to run their lives more successfully. I began to offer training courses, which were immediately successful and have proved highly popular. Today **TRIM** has improved the lives of thousands of people across the world.

NOW IT'S YOUR TURN! LET'S GET ON.

Chapter Two

Overview

INFORMATION

MANAGEMENT

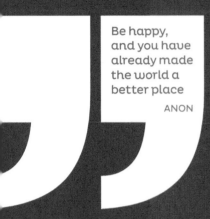

> Be happy,
> and you have
> already made
> the world a
> better place
>
> ANON

THE FIRST STEP IS UNDERSTANDING THE PROBLEM

You would not be reading this book unless you had already decided that you want to make some changes to improve your life. But before we start thinking about the way you would like things to be, let's begin by taking a look at the way you're living your life right now. This will help you to identify the areas of activity where you are reasonably happy with the way things are going (always good for morale!) and the aspects of life where you really see problems and want to make progress.

Most people divide their lives between four main 'zones'

UNDERSTANDING
THE PROBLEM

THE TRIM SYSTEM

FIVE STEPS TO A
BETTER LIFE

Of course these spaces may overlap. The boundaries shift as life moves on, and for some people the lines between the zones may be difficult to draw. How about you? Maybe, if you are not formally employed but spend your time looking after young children, you might think that 'work' and 'family' are the same. Are they really? Babies are wonderful and most of the time looking after them is a joy. But there are aspects of childcare – the inevitable mess, interminable laundry, constant need to prepare food – that would look pretty much like 'work' if you were doing them for someone other than your own delightful kids.

If you're really lucky, you might find it hard to distinguish between 'work' and 'leisure' – maybe your passion in life is photography and you have become a professional photographer. Does that necessarily mean that you would choose to give up every weekend to photograph weddings, or voluntarily spend your time taking portraits of other people's little darlings? Probably not...

The point is that all these different areas of interest constantly demand more and more from us – and, often, they want it now! The pressures build up – to be in two places at once, to try to get more done in less time. Eventually, you are liable to end up satisfying the needs of everyone but yourself. 'Work' takes up the biggest part of most people's waking lives: for many it's the place they would least like to be, but it's essential to provide the means to enjoy the other zones. But some people are really fulfilled at work and gain direct benefits from it in the three other zones. Ultimately, we all want to have all the zones working in harmony. This is what **TRIM** will help you to do.

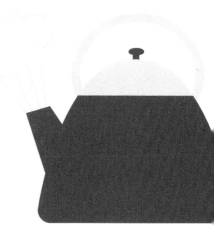

THE TRIM SYSTEM
So – what are you signing up for?

As you go through the book we'll look at the four main influences on just about everything you do

TIME
– how you make the most of it

RELATIONSHIPS
– how you handle them so that everyone benefits
(most of all you!)

INFORMATION
– how you organise it so that it's there whenever
you need it

MANAGEMENT
– how you blend together the other three
elements to produce a perfect result (for you)

TIME

It's a cliché, but it's true – you can't manage time. Rich or poor, weak or powerful, we all get 24 hours in a day, 365 days in a year, and there's nothing we can ever do to change that.

What we can do – and what has spawned a whole industry over the last 80 years – is to get better at allocating our time. You can look at this from two directions: either we want to get what needs to be done, done in as little time as possible – or we would like to spend as much time as we can doing what we want to do, not what others want us to do. You might think these come to the same thing! But **TRIM** ensures that, even when you have to do things which you would avoid if you could, you will be satisfied that you have made a choice and decided that you are doing what is best for you in the circumstances – because it best meets your own personal objectives at that specific point in time.

You can't buy time, but of course some people have more choice about how to spend it than others. If you are rich enough, you may decide to pay somebody to spend their time doing the chores in your garden – but maybe still wish that you could be outside pruning your roses instead of sitting in a stuffy office. Maybe you can afford a Ferrari – but never have the leisure time to drive it. Many high-powered people are 'money rich and time poor', while those who retired on a modest pension are often 'time rich but money poor'. Whatever your circumstances, you will have to make decisions about how you spend your time which will be just as important to your quality of life as decisions on how you spend your money. Sometimes there will be a trade-off between the two: take the bus and save money, or take the plane and save time?

As you progress through the book you will see that choices about what you do with your time are at the heart of how you live your life. If you get these decisions right, you are well on the way to maximising your personal efficiency and effectiveness.

RELATIONSHIPS

Unless you are a hermit, you probably 'relate' to dozens of other people every day of your life. You may see members of your family at breakfast (a dangerous time of day – the Royal Air Force club in London used to set its breakfast tables facing the wall, to spare members the stress of having to make polite conversation too early in the morning!) You may meet people on your way to work, in your office, socially, in shops, pubs, or sports clubs. You'll speak to them face-to-face, on the phone, by email, text or on social networking sites. Your 'relationships' may range from simple courtesies as you buy a newspaper, through 'strictly business' phonecalls to intimate conversations with family or friends.

What's for sure is that your relationships with other people are what define life – not just for you, but often for them too. Your relationship with people gives them the window they see you through, so your life will be more pleasant if you make sure that they like what they see!

The tools and techniques which you will learn here are designed to help you handle your relationships so that you are confident that you are doing what's best for yourself, while always taking other people's interests and values into account.

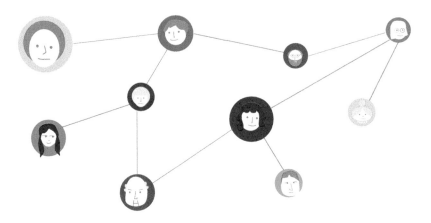

INFORMATION

We'll be talking a lot about information throughout the book. You're bombarded with it from dawn to dusk – actually, in just about every waking moment – and learning how to organise it is the key to being able to control your life. Information management gets its own section later, but almost all of the **TRIM** tools and techniques are concerned with it in one way or another.

The simple fact is that even the supercomputer which is your brain can't process and store all of the information flooding in. The only way to make sure that things are properly dealt with – remembered, stored, retrieved and acted on – is to help your brain, and specifically your memory, by doing a bit of the work yourself.

Think of something we all have to do – the supermarket shop. Normally it's not the kind of experience that you want to repeat too often, so most people try to pick up enough supplies to keep the household going for a week or so. Now, it is easy enough to work out the essential elements: fruit, vegetables, meat, milk, frozen food, bit of booze, and so on. But how about the other bits? A battery for the smoke alarm that started beeping on Thursday? Chocolates for Auntie Maud's birthday, which you remembered at ten o'clock on Tuesday night? Sticky tape, because the roll ran out on Wednesday? Sure, your brain will remind you of all these things – but it's very unlikely to be in the shop, where you can actually do something about them! Much more likely that you will remember in the car on the way home...

The answer, of course, is a shopping list which you can add to as soon as something runs out or occurs to you. This way you are helping your brain by getting information out of it and into a format which is convenient and easy for you to use. Of course this is a simple example, and some of the information problems you face will be more complex – but one of the joys of **TRIM** is that most of its principles are refreshingly simple. We'll explore lots of other ways of controlling the information storm and making it useful instead of just daunting.

MANAGEMENT

I define 'management' as being the skill of combining the information you have, the relationships which you are part of and the time you have available to ensure that you consistently achieve the most advantageous outcome for yourself. In fact, if you have the information and the relationships right, the management will pretty much look after itself – but the **TRIM** tools provide a simple and reliable way of making sure everything fits together properly. This is the best way of persauding others to give more than they would otherwise give in the pursuit of achieving your goals – or if you like, getting them to do what you want them to do!

Look at it another way. Let's say you want to meet some friends in the pub on Wednesday evening. To make this work, you have to mix in all the elements above. First, you need to check that you have no other commitments that evening – and maybe that the rest of your family doesn't have any plans that affect you. That's 'time'. Then you'll want to find out if your chums are free and would like to get together. That's 'relationships'. Finally, 'information': you need to choose the pub and the time to meet, and make sure you tell everyone else. 'Management' means pulling all these different bits together so that all the arrangements work with no problems.

Of course I'm not suggesting that you need to go through a routine to complete all these steps, simply to fix a visit to the pub. In a simple case like this, your brain does them all automatically and you hardly even need to think about it. But real life produces much more complex problems, all the time, and it is often helpful to be able to break them down into manageable bits which you can solve individually and then stitch back together. This is what **TRIM** helps you to do.

EFFICIENCY AND EFFECTIVENESS

All the way through this book, I'll be talking about two qualities that **TRIM** is designed to make central in your life – efficiency and effectiveness. Because it's important to understand what I mean by these two words, let's look at them now.

'Efficiency' is about getting things done. So in **TRIM** terms, it means doing what you said you would do, never letting people down, never forgetting things you have committed to do. Being efficient is absolutely essential if you want to achieve your goals – but it's not enough! To really make an impression you need to be not only efficient, but effective too.

EFFICIENT
Keeping the balls
in the air

INEFFICIENT
Doh!

EFFECTIVE
The Mona Lisa

INEFFECTIVE
Not the Mona Lisa!

'Effectiveness' is about not only doing things, but using your abilities to accomplish them in the best possible way – the most useful, the most timely, the most economical in terms of time and money. Effectiveness is the result of combining all of your decisions about how you use your time and your abilities, to maximise the outcome for your and other people's benefit. If 'efficiency' equals 'quantity', then 'effectiveness' equals 'quality' – and it is by effectiveness that you will be measured and judged by your family, friends and colleagues.

FIVE STEPS TO A BETTER LIFE
The practical links between motivation & achievement

Everything I am going to tell you will help you to do five things which, between them, will enable you to manage your life:

END
Achievement of your goals

5.
Negotiate the best possible outcomes in discussions with your friends and colleagues

4.
Store and manage information so you can always find it and use it

3.
Plan and monitor how you allocate your resources of time and ability

START
Motivation

2.
Decide on your priorities

1.
Work out what you really want to achieve – now, next week, next year and even further ahead

All of these activities will become second nature, and as you become more familiar with the **TRIM** tools and techniques you will find yourself doing them almost without thinking.

WORK OUT WHAT YOU REALLY WANT TO ACHIEVE

In the next chapter we will look at why you need goals, and the sort of targets that you should be setting yourself for different timescales, in different areas of your life. You'll learn how we all have different kinds of ambitions, and how to set objectives that will give you a good measure of how well you are doing in running other aspects of your life. Reviewing and modifying your goals to take account of developments is a vital part of the process.

2 **DECIDE ON YOUR PRIORITIES**

Priorities are different from objectives – sometimes very different – but you can't have one without the other. Very often you will have to think about your priorities to decide what you are going to do, who you are going to see, or whether you will make a commitment to someone. People have very personal ways of establishing their priorities, depending on their own work style and approach to life: but **TRIM** will make sure that however you decide on them, your priorities work for you. You will learn how to deliver on your commitments, every time – by controlling what you commit yourself to. If this sounds a bit hard-nosed, relax – you can keep all your promises, but still never need to say 'no' to anything other people ask you to do!

 PLAN AND MONITOR YOUR ACTIVITIES

TRIM's two main tools ensure that you always know exactly what's coming up, and what you should be doing about it.

The first and most important is the Terrain Map. The Terrain Map provides a dynamic picture of all of your commitments, contacts, travel and tasks for the day, which is constantly updated as you deal with new information and progress through the day's activities. It provides the central focus for everything that happens during the day and ensures that you always know exactly where you should be, what you should be doing or who you should be talking to, and what information you need to have at hand to make your activities as effective as possible.

You'll learn how to put your personal Terrain Map together and adapt it to work for you – and then how to keep it updated and current so that it can be used as a guide and reference throughout the day.

The other vital tool is the **Weekly Helicopter Trip** – a regular review of the past week's events and an initial planner for the next two weeks. This helicopter view sets everything in context and ensures no major clashes: it gives you a real feeling of empowerment when you know exactly where you plan to be and what you will be able to achieve. Of course innumerable things will happen in that time – some of them predictable (so plan!) and some right out of the blue. But having an overall picture of the way things should look is a great basis to work from!

As you work through the book you will learn how to plan effectively and how to monitor the way your plans are unfolding. You'll also discover the power of mental visualisation and mental rehearsal for your meetings and negotiations.

4 **STORE AND MANAGE YOUR INFORMATION SO THAT YOU CAN ALWAYS FIND IT AND USE IT**

First we'll look at how people communicate, and I'll suggest the most effective ways of storing the information this produces so that it always relates to the right people or actions, and can easily be retrieved when you need it. **TRIM's** information systems are all about capturing the opportunities – setting up ways of sorting the mass of information you're constantly bombarded with, recognising the valuable bits and making sure that they get put where they are automatically connected to other relevant 'stuff' and don't just disappear or wither away.

Chapter 4 also deals with commitments and promises – you make them all the time, whether it's to get a report done, meet a friend for coffee or watch your son playing football – and the way you deal with them is the main yardstick against which your friends and colleagues judge you. Do you always do what you say you will? Or are you unreliable – late for appointments, if you turn up at all, and always missing the deadline for urgent reports?

TRIM provides foolproof ways of making sure that you always carry out your undertakings – on time – or, if it is really impossible for you to do so, of reaching new agreements that leave all parties feeling satisfied. And never forgetting an appointment again...

5   NEGOTIATE THE BEST POSSIBLE OUTCOMES WITH YOUR FRIENDS AND COLLEAGUES

Does 'negotiate' sound a bit formal? After all, you don't sit round a conference table to decide which pub to go to after the tennis match. But in fact, you're almost certainly negotiating every time you make arrangements with someone: you and they probably have slightly different preferences ("It's closer to my house..." or "I can take the bus and leave the car at home...") and you will almost certainly end up making a commitment ("See you at three..."). Of course in the work context you may be making much more important decisions – and commitments. So it pays to understand your relationships and make sure that you always have the information you need at your fingertips. That way you can manage your interactions, get the outcomes that suit you and have others deliver for you.

As always, there may be many considerations in your negotiations and things may not be as simple as they appear. You might decide that it's not worth arguing with your teenage son about making dinner tonight, because you know that next week you'll be asking him to walk the dog while you're away. So a tactical retreat is called for... you decide to give up a short-term objective in favour of a longer-term one.

And that will take us nicely on to the first essential of the TRIM system – working out what you really want to do with your life, and when. READ ON...

Now you know what **TRIM** will be doing, let's finish this overview off by having a look at what you're starting with. Think about the four 'zones' of your life – Work, Leisure, Family, and Self. Then use the template on the next page to note down which of your activities fit into which category. Now think where the overlaps are, and the conflicts. It's not a test! There are no marks, and indeed no right or wrong answers. But if you are honest with yourself you'll find that you have quite a good picture of the way your life works now. You'll know the areas where you're pretty satisfied with the way things are going – and the ones where you'd definitely like to see some improvements.

ZONES

WORK

LEISURE
friends & outside interests

FAMILY

SELF

JACK	JILL
Breakfast. Expect the bus will be late as always – still, don't think there's much on first thing. Looks a bit cold – jeans and thick jacket weather.	Breakfast and a quick look at the **Terrain Map**. Ah – possibly difficult meeting at 11.00 with Brian from Head Office. Better wear something a bit smart and arrive in plenty of time. Still, lunch with Jane will be fun. Clare arriving this evening so must buy stuff for dinner.
Still on the bus. Should have remembered those roadworks snarling up the traffic.	Got time to make a few phonecalls before people disappear into meetings. **Terrain Map** has phone numbers and a quick reminder of the points to discuss.
Damn. Completely forgot that Brian from HO is arriving for a meeting. Wish I'd worn a suit... Better have a look at the papers – I think they're in my Pending tray. Wonder what that call from Jill was about? Must give her a call back after the meeting.	Got the agenda done for tomorrow's Budget Committee – just sent it off for agreement from George. Ah – email from Jack asking for copies of the papers for our meeting with Brian – had them on my desk so I scanned them and sent them to him. He says he'll call me after the meeting – pity, because I was going to invite him for a chat before Brian arrives.
I'd been rather counting on using this morning to finish off that paper I'm supposed to be giving Stuart this afternoon – maybe just got time to get it done before Brian arrives. I can pretty much remember what 's in the meeting papers anyway.	Time to have another look through the papers and think about what I want to get out of this meeting – and what Brian is likely to be looking for too. I'm pretty sure he'll try to get Jack to move to the Glasgow office – which could actually solve some problems for me. I'll give him discreet support. Jack will probably resist initially, but I think he'll realise that it will offer him some opportunities – if he gets his act together and organises his life!
Where is my notebook? Why does the damn thing always hide when I need it? Going to be late...	Time for a few words to find out how Brian's daughter is getting on – **Terrain Map** reminds me he told me that she broke her arm a couple of weeks ago.

And so on....

Goals

> If you don't know where you're goin', you'll end up someplace else. YOGI BERRA

THE TRIM COURSE IS ALL ABOUT HELPING YOU TO MAKE THE MOST OF YOUR 'JOURNEY THROUGH LIFE'

– how to be better organised, completely reliable, more valued by other people, and generally happy with the way you live.

But you can only make a journey if you have somewhere to go! There is no point in travelling at top speed if you're going in the wrong direction – and no satisfaction in being efficient and effective at doing something if you don't know why you're doing it in the first place.

So this chapter is all about deciding where you want to go in life, when you would like to arrive and how you will know how close you are to getting there.

GOAL-SETTING

WHAT DOES A 'GOAL' LOOK LIKE?

WHEN DO YOU NEED TO SET LOWER-LEVEL GOALS?

WHAT KIND OF LOWER-LEVEL GOALS?

WHAT HAPPENS IF YOU MISS YOUR GOALS?

GOAL-SETTING

If you work in an office or factory, you will already be familiar – probably all too familiar! – with the idea of 'goal-setting'. Organisations set goals, or targets, to measure how much work they are getting done. Often, individual workers or teams are given incentives to encourage them to hit these targets – or even penalties if they don't. Goals like this are useful for the organisations concerned, but their employees often see them as simply an extra pressure to work harder!

The goals that you are going to set for yourself are completely different, for one very important reason:

they are about YOU and YOU alone – YOUR hopes, YOUR ambitions, YOUR dreams

Nobody can tell you what goals you should set for yourself. This is the time when you decide what you really want to get from life, or achieve in life – and at this stage you're just choosing your destinations, not trying to work out how you will get to them.

Let's look at how you might make your choices.

WHAT DOES A 'GOAL' LOOK LIKE?

Some goals are easily defined – like in football: ball goes into the back of the net, goal scored, end of story. Sporting goals are usually easily measurable: get my golf handicap into single figures, run 10K in under an hour, ski down a black run without falling over.

You can also set physical goals so you know when you have achieved them – lose 5kg, stop smoking, manage 50 press-ups.

All of these have a place – we all need to have these kinds of goals, and we'll talk about them later in this chapter. You'll feel good when you hit the targets. But are they enough to live your life by?

I think not. What you need is an ultimate goal – something like the North Pole, which will constantly attract your life's compass, so that you can always tell whether you are heading in the right direction to reach it. Your North Pole Goal will be something that you know you're not going to attain easily, or (probably) quickly. It will be your life's ambition, which you really want to fulfil and are prepared to work towards patiently and consistently. Many of the decisions you take in your life will be made on the basis of 'Will this bring me closer to my North Pole Goal? Which way is the compass telling me to go?' When you reach it, you will feel a massive sense of achievement. You will be able to say,

> I have been working
> all my life for this!

What sort of thing do people aspire to as their North Pole Goal? If you ask most people what their ultimate ambition would be, they will often say immediately that they want to go on a round-the-world holiday, or drive a Rolls Royce, or simply 'be stinking rich'. OK – for some individuals these things might genuinely be the pinnacle of their lives. But usually, when they have reflected for a while, people modify their answers. Instead of 'one-off' adventures or experiences, or general states like being rich, they have rather deeper desires. 'I would like to make sure my family's future is secure', 'I would like to be able to grow old comfortably', or 'I want to feel that I have really helped someone'.

It's worth just pondering for a while to work out what your aim in life really is. Like most people, you would probably like to be rich. But why? Just being rich isn't much fun (so I'm told!) It's what you do with the money that can give you the satisfaction. Try thinking beyond the 'rich' bit and work out what you would really like to do if you could. Maybe you should aim for that instead! Do you really want to drive a Rolls Royce – or just enjoy the admiration of the people who see you behind the wheel? Maybe you could earn their esteem in a different way!

WHEN DO YOU NEED TO SET LOWER-LEVEL GOALS?

As well as your North Pole Goal you will want to set yourself many others, ranging from important and long-term ('be in charge of the department by my 30th birthday') to minor and close up ('get the grass cut before the football starts on telly'). Some of these may be important steps towards the North Pole Goal – you'll only accept them if your 'life compass' tells you that you will be going in the right direction! Others simply help to get your life in order: various psychological studies have shown that people who consistently make progress towards defined goals are not only much more effective but happier than those who don't.

How many targets you set, and the way you work towards them, will depend a bit on how organised a person you are.

Type A
If you are happiest when you know exactly what you have to do, and by when, then you will probably want to set lots of goals in all sorts of areas of your life – working, studying, sports, even going on holiday! You may find that you get real satisfaction from being able to tick your achievements off a list, and be comfortable because you always know just how well you're progressing in your different activities. You will end up with a sort of 'pyramid of goals', with your North Pole Goal at the top and each level underneath representing smaller and smaller targets that you need to hit to achieve your lifetime goal.

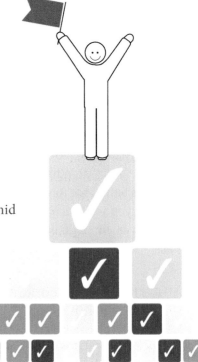

Type B

If you are a person who doesn't like to be too tied down by deadlines and 'milestones', but prefers just to know that you're making progress, your approach may be completely different. In this case you will probably want some general goals which reassure you that you're moving in the right direction. But you may have only a few specific targets in important areas where you have decided that even you need to monitor your progress carefully.

As with most lifestyle choices, there's no right way or wrong way of goal-setting. You should end up with whatever suits your style and gives you the best results. The best way is to try a few different systems and see what works for you.

A word of warning: there are people who end up spending much of their time obsessively setting targets, monitoring progress and reviewing priorities. They create lifetime plans, five-year plans, one-year plans, one-month plans, daily targets...

...this is not what life is for!

Goals should make your life simpler and help motivate you to achieve what you want – if they impose new and unwanted burdens, they are the wrong goals.

WHAT KIND OF LOWER-LEVEL GOALS?

Your North Pole Goal will always be the main 'guiding light' for the really big decisions in your life. As long as it remains valid, as a true expression of what you genuinely want to achieve, it's very unlikely that you will ever decide to do something which will take you further away from this goal. But because it is so far in the future, there probably won't be very many decisions you need to make which are directly related to the North Pole Goal. As we discussed above, you will need to have lower-level goals.

Suppose your North Pole Goal is to lead a team to climb Mount Everest. To achieve this, you are going to have to:

✓ make a lot of money

✓ be a good fundraiser

✓ be physically fit

✓ be an expert climber on rock, snow and ice

✓ be a good organiser and administrator

✓ maybe make decisions about your family life

So to achieve your overall goal of leading the Everest expedition, you will first have to reach lower level targets in all of these areas.

The kind of goals you want to set will vary, depending on your own lifestyle and conditions, and on the North Pole Goal you have set yourself to work towards. Here are a few areas you might consider:

Career

Are you ambitious? How far up the ladder do you want to go? You might be able to get to the top – but that will mean sacrifices in other areas, so be realistic and think about what else you're prepared to give up to succeed in your career!

Financial

How much money do you need to earn to achieve your North Pole Goal? Can you do that in your present job, or do you need to think again about your career?

Education

Is there something you would really like to learn about? Do you want to learn a language? If you need to change your job, do you need to gain new qualifications?

Family

Do you want to be a parent? If so, what ambitions do you have about the way your children will be brought up and educated? What opportunities would you like them to have?

Lifestyle

If your North Pole Goal involves you being around for a while, now could be the time to set some goals for losing weight, stopping smoking or drinking a bit less. More broadly, are you happy with the way you're living? Maybe you want to move to a bigger house, or avoid a two-hour commute to work – these could be very worthwhile targets.

Sports and physical

If you're in training or go to the gym, you will already have plenty of targets and goals! Even if you just want to improve your golf handicap or get more first serves in, goal-setting will help to motivate you and let you monitor your progress.

Community

Would you like to contribute by volunteering or helping to run local facilities? How are you going to make the world a better place?

Pleasure

Of course you're allowed time off from all these goal-driven activities – but even then, you might want to set yourself some targets in your hobbies!

Inevitably many of these areas may overlap: attaining your financial goals will probably be much easier if you are also achieving your career targets. The overlapping ones are easy. What is more difficult is when your goals in different areas come into conflict. For example, one of the sacrifices you might have to make to be a career high-flyer could be having to give up your place in your beloved football team – or, if you want to have a family, you might need to put changing your job on hold.

In the end, it all comes down to the North Pole Goal. You can only look at the choices you have to make, and decide which ones are going to be most helpful in moving you towards your ultimate ambition.

The answers will usually be pretty self-evident.

SETTING YOUR GOALS

There are a few basic guidelines for goal-setting, and a classic acronym to help. All of your goals should be **SMART**:

SPECIFIC: you need to be as exact as possible about what you want to achieve. Don't decide that you want to be 'comfortable in retirement' – aim 'to own my house and have an income of £2000 a month'.

MEASURABLE: you need to know how well you're doing. It's easier if you can quantify the result you're looking for. So not 'have a decent amount saved up when I'm 60' – go for 'have £40,000 in the bank when I'm 60'.

ACTIONABLE: try to have 'action' verbs rather than just 'being' verbs. Not 'have fun with my friends' – 'get in touch with at least one friend every week'.

REALISTIC: this is a difficult one! Your North Pole Goal should be something you really want, which you absolutely can't do now. People do astonishing things: think of the South African Mark Shuttleworth, who always wanted to go into space, and doggedly made enough money to do so! So who is to judge what is realistic as a goal, and what is simply a pipedream? I would say that your North Pole Goal should be something that you believe you can achieve if you are prepared to work for it. Nothing that anyone else thinks, matters. Your lower level goals should stretch you but certainly not be impossible – just think how depressing it would be to constantly miss your targets simply because they were always out of range!

TIMEBOUND: many of the goals you will set in life will have very specific deadlines or 'delivery dates' – and in fact, it's essential that they do, or they become dreams rather than objectives. But it may be a bit different for your North Pole Goal: depending what it is, you might want to achieve it by the time you have children, or when you're 50, or when you retire – or even just to let it be as a target to aim for until you finally hit it!

It is important to write down your goals. When you commit them to paper – or even to your computer – you are making a real statement of intent, and you'll feel that you are making a start.

Writing your goals down also means that you can take the other essential action – reviewing them. Re-reading them and considering your progress (remember 'Measurable'?) gives you a reality check and reassures you that you are moving forward and not just chasing dreams. How often you review your goals will depend on their timescale: there's not much point in reassessing progress towards your North Pole Goal every week, but if you have to research and write a report by the end of the month a weekly review might be essential. Your review can also help identify the next step you need to take to hit the target – and later in this book, you'll learn how to incorporate this into **TRIM** tools like the Terrain Map and the **Weekly Helicopter Trip**.

My goals...

WHAT HAPPENS IF YOU MISS YOUR GOALS?

First of all, it's important to remember that everyone misses goals from time to time. Goals are there to help us improve our performance. If we all hit them all the time, the only thing that would show is that the goals were set too low!

So, when you miss your target, the first thing to do is to work out why. If you had a short-term goal of losing 3kg before September, and you ended up losing only 2kg, why did this happen? In this very simple example there are all sorts of possible explanations: you were on a gourmet food-tasting holiday for two weeks in July, you started working in a chocolate factory in June, you attended four weddings in August.... (we are all good at rationalising excuses for not quite making weight-loss targets!) But think more deeply, beyond the easy explanations. Did you miss the target because you just weren't motivated enough to achieve it? After all, even if you were tempted by delicious calories being available, you could always have been strong and turned them down! Or were there other, less obvious reasons? Overeating is often related to internal stress. Were you worried, or depressed, about something?

The important point is that not achieving your target gives you an opportunity to relate it to other areas of your life. If you missed it simply because you didn't care enough to work towards it – what will you do? Just resetting it for another 3 months down the line won't do any good, unless you look honestly at your own motivation and decide that this time you really do want to do the hard graft and find the willpower.

If missing the target was due to some internal factor – like unhappiness or depression – then reviewing your progress is a good time to recognise this and decide what you can do to make things better. But again, don't just re-set the target without doing anything about the underlying reasons you missed it this time – that will just make you even more unhappy. Take the opportunity to find help, and don't set another target until you are sure you're really ready to tackle it.

Of course there are often completely unpredictable reasons why goals are not achieved. Illness, sudden lifestyle changes, bereavement, family problems, accidents – all the things the insurance companies like to call 'acts of God' can make it quite impossible to hit your targets. In this case, the only thing to do is to work out whether these are long-term or short-term effects, see how they affect other targets including your North Pole Goal, and go back to the drawing board!

Or, finally, it may be that you simply set your goal unrealistically high. If this is the case, it doesn't matter in the least that you missed it – and you have gained useful information about the progress you are able to make. With this new knowledge you will be able to set a revised target which you are absolutely sure you can reach – so long as you try hard enough!

drawing board

WHAT ABOUT TARGETS THAT YOU REACH EARLY, OR TOO EASILY?

Sometimes you will find that you attain your goal much sooner than you expected, or 'too easily' – when you were expecting to have to try very hard to get there, you suddenly realise that you have arrived!

Though this might feel quite comfortable, it's not necessarily a good thing! Research has shown (surprise, surprise...) that difficult goals not only improve performance more than easy goals, but also lead to a much greater feeling of satisfaction when they are achieved.

As with missing your goals, there are many possible explanations – changed circumstances, improved performance or simply setting the target too low. Again, whatever the reason, you have a great opportunity to re-assess the situation and make the changes you need. And when you reach your North Pole Goal, it's time to set another one.

If you find yourself regularly outperforming your expectations, the answer is obvious – be more ambitious! You can do it....

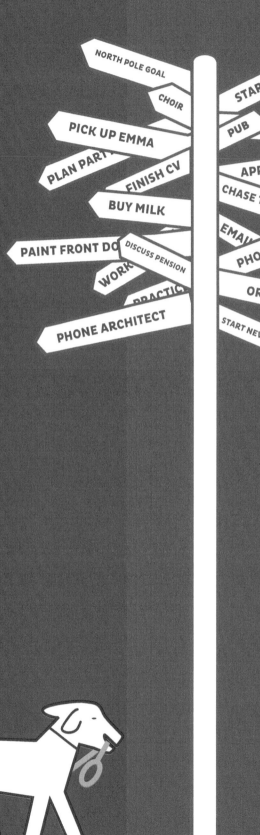

Priorities

HELP!

NOW!

URGENT

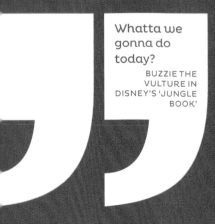

Whatta we gonna do today?

BUZZIE THE VULTURE IN DISNEY'S 'JUNGLE BOOK'

GOALS AND PRIORITIES

So – you have your goals and targets all sorted out. Great! Now you know what you really want to achieve. You've set out various routes to take you in the right direction, measure progress and give you the satisfaction of celebrating solid achievements.

What comes next? I mean, what are you actually going to do *now*? Obviously, you can't work towards all your goals at once. And anyway, you've got to prepare for a meeting tomorrow morning – and you were thinking of going to the gym, or maybe having a couple of pints with the lads...

Ah.... so many possibilities, so many things you need to do! Congratulations – you have discovered why we all need PRIORITIES.

Many people think that priorities are the same as goals. After all, we have some goals which we know are really important, and others which we are prepared to leave for a while – doesn't this automatically set priorities for us? Well, no it doesn't.

At this stage we need to look at the difference between something that is important and something that is urgent. Important things – tasks, goals, ambitions – *stay* important: if you need good exam results so you can go to university, that is probably a critically important goal, both for your happiness over the next few years and as a step towards your North Pole goal. However, it is unlikely to be *urgent*: unless you have an essay to finish or a test tomorrow, you probably don't have to do anything about it straight away. Getting good results is important but not urgent.

On the other hand, some tasks can be urgent but not important. Incoming phone calls, routine meetings, casual visitors, social invitations, office birthday parties, getting home in time to watch a TV show – all of these things, and a thousand others, may impose deadlines or require immediate attention. But in the greater scheme of things, none of them is likely to be very important.

A sensible method of setting priorities is the only way to deal with this rampaging pack of 'things to do' demanding our time and attention. Without priorities, we become 'reactors' – responding to demands and developments as they come up, unable to postpone or refuse tasks and getting very little satisfaction from completing them. Without priorities the steering fails: we lose control completely, becoming event-driven and directionless. Instead of leaving a neat line of goals achieved and targets met, our wake will be littered with the wreckage of unfinished projects, unfulfilled commitments and disappointed people.

There is another very important difference between goals and priorities. As we saw in the last chapter, we decide our own goals. Other people (such as our employers!) may set targets for us to aim at: but ultimately, it's up to us to decide whether to accept them or not. Our own goals all lead us towards the ultimate North Pole Goal – or there's no point in having them.

Priorities are different. Our priorities can be changed by all sorts of events, and by decisions made by other people. Accidents and illnesses happen, children are born, people die. You may win the lottery! Any of these, and many others you can think of from your own experience, can change priorities dramatically.

Sometimes we have little choice but to fit in with other people's timings. We can't choose what time we need to be at the airport to catch a flight, or the time of a meeting involving many other people. Kids have to be collected when school finishes – not half an hour later. In these cases we simply have to fit in, or change our plans dramatically – and either of these options is likely to influence the priorities of other things we're trying to do.

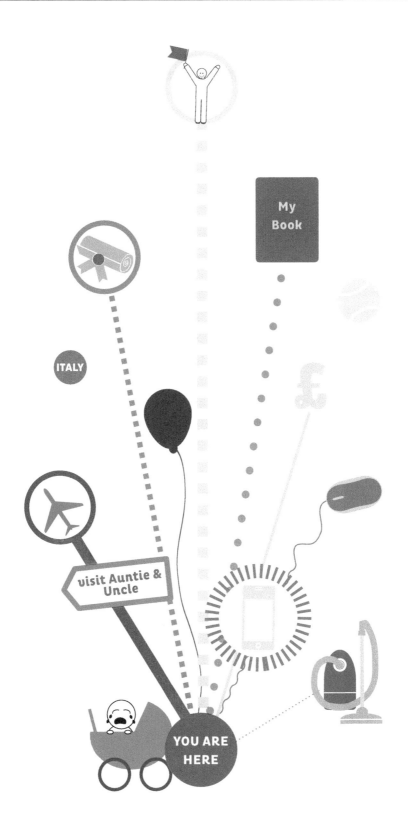

KEYS TO SETTING PRIORITIES

When we talked about goals, we saw that different people have different approaches to the number of goals they need and how often they need to review them. The same is true for priority setting.

Some people like to find excuses for putting off difficult tasks until the last minute. Writers are particularly prone to this: when the famous American humorist H L Mencken was being pursued by his publisher, who sent telegrams demanding to know when he would finish a long-overdue manuscript, he eventually cabled back 'When I have finished cleaning my tennis shoes'. For people like this, the temptation is always to find 'displacement activities' – small, often trivial tasks that give the impression of activity, but simply provide a way of postponing the thing that actually matters. The technical term for this is 'procrastination' – and procrastinators need to recognise the problems they are making for themselves and prioritise their tasks accordingly.

Other people, often those who are happiest if they have lots of day-to-day goals, like to have a constant flow of small victories to keep them going. The problem is that, rather like procrastinators, these 'nibblers' tend to get all the small jobs done to give the impression of progress, and never get on to the bigger ones.

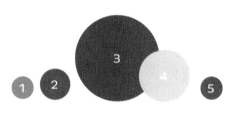

Then finally, there are people who like to take a rational and analytical approach to running their lives – the ones who look at each task as it arises and assign it a value so that they can do things in the most logical order.

Let's look at these in turn and see how they might approach priority setting.

Procrastinators

William James, one of the founders of modern psychology, said "Nothing is so fatiguing as the eternal hanging on of an uncompleted task". I think we have all occasionally been guilty of avoiding the difficult task of the day and getting on with easier distractions – but always knowing that, sooner or later, we'd have to knuckle down and get to grips with what we've spent time and energy trying to escape! It's not a good feeling and it really does sap the will to get on with useful things.

The classic method of defeating procrastination was set out in Brian Tracy's famous book 'Eat That Frog!' His theory was allegedly adapted from an old folk saying, that if every morning you started the day by eating a live frog, then the worst was over and nothing so bad could happen to you for the rest of the day. (This certainly sounds true – but a little extreme!)

Tracy says that the equivalent of the frog for most people is the biggest, hardest, least appealing task on their 'to-do' list – the one that they are most likely to find excuses to put off. If, instead of avoiding it, you tackle it straight away, first thing, you will often find that it is much easier than you feared – and you will feel liberated and energised to get on with your other activities for the rest of the day. Sounds like a good theory....

Nibblers

Nibblers are a bit like procrastinators – they also tend to shy away from the bigger tasks on the list, but for different reasons. Rather than trying to get away from something potentially unpleasant, they are anxious that by tackling difficult tasks they will fail to complete them and therefore lack a measurable achievement – and so have nothing to tick off. The temptation is to cherry-pick small, easily completed tasks and ignore the bigger ones.

The trouble with this technique is that it's too easy to fill up all the time in the day with little, unimportant tasks which masquerade as real work but eventually leave no time for the bigger stuff. So not only do the things that actually matter not get done, but you end up feeling tired – and frustrated because you know that, really, you have achieved nothing!

The only way to deal with the problem is to recognise it. If you are honest with yourself you know very well which are the genuinely important tasks you need to tackle. Each morning, when you look at your **Things to Do** or your Terrain Map (we'll be explaining about these and your stacks soon!), go through the tasks you want to complete during the day and highlight the three most important ones. Then, as soon as your other commitments give you time, go for them! Take the most important first and don't stop until you have finished it, or can't get any further. Then move on to the next most important. When you have had a good go at all three, you can start on the less important (and maybe more fun!) stuff.

TASK A	TASK F
TASK B	TASK G
TASK C	TASK H
TASK D	TASK I
TASK E	TASK J

Of course, you might not get everything done – and some of the unimportant tasks may be delayed for ages. But the point is that this shouldn't matter – if it does, you can always move them up the 'important' list!

If, at the end of the day, things remain undone, then you will have the satisfaction of knowing that you couldn't have fitted everything in anyway – and the important things got done. There isn't much satisfaction in knowing that you have managed to tidy up your sock drawer, if you didn't get round to making the cake for your daughter's birthday party this evening...

Analysts

Some people are able to take a very detached view of their priority setting and assign a 'value' to each task. These 'analysts' like to know that they are always working on the most important thing they could be doing, any time all the time. The classic way of doing this was described by Steven Covey, with what has become known as a 'Covey Quadrant':

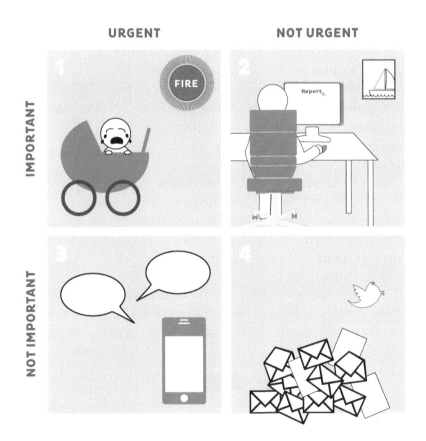

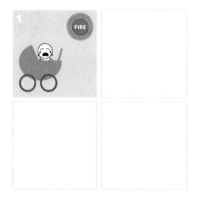

1. IMPORTANT & URGENT

The principle is obvious: tasks range from 'Important and Urgent' down to 'Not Important and Not Urgent'. The Important and Urgent ones are usually things over which we have no control, but have to respond to straight away: you can think of your own examples of events or situations which you know immediately simply have to take precedence over everything else that's going on. For most of us, fortunately, these crises are few and far between: but if you are on a Lifeboat crew, or a part-time fireman – or a mother with small children – you know they are going to happen and you just have to adapt your other activities to accommodate this. Sometimes, of course, we bring them on ourselves – most of the time we should be able to avoid impending deadlines by planning ahead and getting work done on time, but every now and again the system doesn't work and what used to be 'Important but Not Urgent' becomes 'Important and Very Urgent Indeed'!

2. IMPORTANT BUT NOT URGENT

The top right section – 'Important but Not Urgent' – is where we all want to spend as much time as possible. This is where we really get into the stuff that matters. These are the things that help us to work towards our own targets, moving us closer to our North Pole Goal. They are also some of the hardest to get down to (or easiest to neglect!), because we have to react to crises or get distracted into dealing with unimportant but attractive activities. Being an analyst, and actually working to the priorities you set, needs quite a lot of willpower!

☑ important
☒ urgent

- writing a paper
- studying for an exam
- planning a wedding
- training
- taking exercise

3. NOT IMPORTANT BUT URGENT

The 'Not Important but Urgent' items – a phonecall from a customer, an unexpected visit from the boss, your computer crashing – are more difficult: most of the time you can't avoid them completely, and they often demand a bit of time before you can decide whether they are important or not. If they turn out to be 'Not Important' – just terminate them as quickly as you can. But do remember that sometimes, for example for the person who 'just drops by' your desk, their business may be important to *them* – so don't be too dismissive! We'll look later at the best ways of dealing with interruptions.

4. NOT IMPORTANT & NOT URGENT

The bottom half of the quadrant is where we risk getting bogged down, in the stuff that prevents us from getting on with what we really want to do. 'Not Important and Not Urgent' things are obvious – the office joker's daily YouTube picks, tidying your desk, chatting to visitors. All these can easily be dealt with, simply by making a conscious effort to ignore them or cut them short.

WHICH ONE ARE YOU?

So – are you a procrastinator, or a nibbler, or an
analyst? The answer, of course, is that you are
all and none. No-one fits any of these categories
exactly: we all have elements of each, in different
proportions and at different times.

We also have our own ideas about what counts
as urgent, and what as important – and about
what we like to do. For many people, going
through figures to complete a VAT return counts
as absolute torture. But for others, it might come
as a blessed relief from the normal daily grind.
Each to their own!

At the end of the day, setting priorities is a
completely individual process. It depends
on your own perceptions, likes and dislikes,
and on the goals that you have set yourself in
life. Priority setting is certainly not an exact
science. I've set out the three classic strategies
above, but the right one for you might be
a mix of all three – or something different
altogether. Try these for size, see how you
get on, and adapt to find the way
that suits your lifestyle best.

You've set your priorities – what can possibly go wrong....?

Once you have finished arranging your tasks and are ready to tackle them, two problems will inevitably arise:

Life happens...

New tasks will come along and need to be fitted in, somewhere in your rankings – and new information will arrive which will affect the priorities you have already set. If you're not careful, you could spend half your time just re-arranging your priorities!

Logic doesn't always win

Your prioritising may be entirely logical and reasonable. However, you may also need to accept that your mind and body might not share the same standards of cold logic – or in other words, you may simply not feel like tackling your list head-on! There are times when the job will be done better if it's left for a while.

MY KEY TO PRIORITY SETTING

The classic approaches to priority setting which I have outlined in this chapter are excellent tools for understanding the problem – and in a perfect world, they would solve it. But as we have seen, the world is not perfect: circumstances change, and we are not computers which constantly act according to perfect logic.

It is important to have a system for setting your priorities, and you should now be able to work out which one suits you best. But it's also important to have the flexibility to absorb new tasks and react to changing circumstances.

In looking at your priority list, always be aware of the constantly changing vista ahead of you. In this turbulent sea, the only beacons which will always be there to guide you are your goals – your North Pole Goal and all of the subsidiary goals which you need to attain on the way. These goals will be important in keeping your priorities straight.

You will also have a whole range of commitments which you need to fulfil, and these will affect your priorities.

But as you look at your priority list – conscious of your commitments, conscious of the time, conscious of your goals – you should look at your tasks and ask yourself one simple question:

If I don't finish this task by the time it is required, to the quality required – how hard will my backside get kicked?

The harder the kicking, the higher the priority!

This technique may not demonstrate the high level of sophistication you might expect in a lifestyle guide like this – but believe me, it works! However, there is one vital thing you need to remember. If you let people down, you can expect your backside to be kicked. But the biggest kicker of all should be yourself. Top of your list should be ensuring that you do not let yourself down – and if this is not the case, you may need to work on your personal motivation.

This questioning of priorities should be an ongoing process throughout the day. Even when you are deeply engaged in a task, be aware of your surroundings and incoming information that is constantly changing the terrain ahead of you.

Of course life isn't about avoiding punishment! The underlying motivation when you are setting your priorities should always be to ensure that you will be doing what is most rewarding and satisfying for you – and what takes you closer to your North Pole Goal.

Why you need to stay light on your feet...

Laura sets her goals well in advance, and then ensures that she achieves them on time, to the quality required.

Her day starts. She has pre-planned the ten jobs that she will complete by the end of the day. She works diligently throughout the day, pacing herself superbly, avoiding all interruptions. At the end of the day she reviews her work, and is delighted to confirm that all the jobs she set herself have been completed, on time and to standard.

WHAT A STAR! WHAT COULD POSSIBLY BE WRONG WITH HER DISCIPLINED AND RIGOROUS APPROACH?

Well, quite a lot, unfortunately. While Laura has been glued to her desk, beavering away in splendid isolation at her highest-priority tasks, life has been going on in the outside world. When she lifts her nose from the grindstone she discovers two major problems:

• Things have been happening 'out there' which should have completely changed the priority of some of the tasks that Laura has been tackling. For example, the report for tomorrow's 9am meeting at the bank is no longer needed – the meeting has been cancelled. An e-mail went out to everyone involved, but Laura didn't want to be distracted by e-mails and hadn't checked them. So all the time spent on the report was wasted, and the figures will have to be completely redone for the rescheduled meeting next Wednesday. Damn!

• Even worse, Laura has missed out on developments which were actually much more important than any of the tasks she spent the day completing. One of her main customers called, asking her to call back. She had avoided the distraction of phone calls all day, so didn't get the message until after the client had gone home. When she called next morning, the customer explained that he had an emergency requirement for a delivery of Laura's premium product the previous day, but when he didn't hear back from Laura he contacted another supplier who was delighted to take on the job – at a lower price...

Remember that Priorities are not gods to be worshipped and obeyed at all times! You should always try to be flexible enough to take account of developments going on around you.

....but not too light!

Simon is also very diligent. He arrives at his desk early, checks his in-tray and starts working on what looks like the best job in the pile – possibly selecting it by applying the 'backside kicking' rule.

About two minutes into this first task, the interruptions start – someone wants something. Simon loves making people happy, so he actions the request straight away. Half an hour into this new task, in comes another interruption – Simon's door is always open! He will listen to any request, and deal with the latest thing asked of him. After all, he is very efficient - he hates making people wait, and knows that his input is indispensable, so he has to do everything NOW!

By the end of the day Simon may feel satisfied or frustrated, depending on how many requests he has been able to deal with – and perhaps how many tasks, if any, he has been able to score off his 'to do' list.

But of course Simon's real effectiveness will be measured by how many of the jobs he has completed have moved him towards his goals – this should have been how he set his priorities for the day. Simon's day has been completely out of control. By jumping around to every request, he will inevitably have let some people down by not completing tasks he had previously undertaken to do. He won't have got any closer to his own goals – or his employer's.

In fact Simon probably hasn't thought through his goals at all, or used them to set priorities for the day. For him 'doing as he was asked' or 'making people happy' is as close as he gets to a goal. Sadly, by having no structure to his activities through the day, he's unlikely to make anyone very happy but will probably have let some people down. Even worse, the people he succeeded in helping today are just as likely to be let down tomorrow when someone else's request gets in first. And finally, because Simon has been jumping from task to task in such a random way, the quality of his output is almost always below what he could have achieved with a more organised approach.

COMMITMENTS

Much of the **TRIM** Course is about Commitments and Promises, and how you deal with these will have a major effect on how you set and handle your priorities.

Every time you agree to do something you are making a commitment – in effect, a promise to the other party that you will do what you say. You can make a commitment to someone, or have one made by someone else on your behalf – perhaps by accepting a deadline.

The spirit of **TRIM** is that you will only make or accept commitments which you are confident you can deliver; and that you will deliver them. Later in the book you will learn that you can always say 'yes' and never say 'no' – and very soon we'll be introducing the **TRIM** tools – the **Weekly Helicopter Trip** and Terrain Maps – which will ensure that you will always be able to deliver on your commitments efficiently and effectively.

However, in the real world we have to accept that it may not always be possible to deliver as you have planned – circumstances change, crises happen, third parties let you down. So we will also look at the consequences of not being able to deliver on your commitments exactly as you expected – and how this can still lead to an outcome which is perfectly acceptable for all concerned.

The three outcomes

When you have made a commitment, there are only three acceptable outcomes:

1. THE JOB IS DONE

This, of course, should always be the result: you deliver, on time and to the right quality. Slightly early is impressive (but not too early – you don't want to build up expectations that you can always deliver ahead of schedule!) Later we will discuss the 'gift of time' that you sometimes receive, and which you can pass on to the lucky person in the form of an agreed early delivery.

2. YOU RENEGOTIATE

This is the critical bit. If you realise that you can't deliver on your commitment on time, you need *immediately* to contact the person to whom the promise has been made. You will need to explain why you can't deliver as previously promised, and suggest an amended arrangement. Then, you negotiate their acceptance and understanding.

With very few exceptions, deadlines are not immovable: *but there is always a price to pay for not meeting them.* Sometimes this may be literally a financial price, and some formal contracts stipulate exactly what this will be. More often, the price is less obvious – it will be to your reputation, your trustworthiness and your value to others. This can be a much higher price to pay than simple money!

The really crucial elements in renegotiating a commitment are speed and honesty. You must get in touch with the other person just as soon as you know you are going to let them down – because that is what you are going to do. Fast action gives them the maximum time to adapt to the new circumstances – and make other arrangements if they need to. You need to be completely honest too – trying to blame some non-existent third party, or inventing a spurious crisis, will catch up with you in the end and certainly won't work twice.

The great thing to remember is that most people are actually inclined to be helpful. If they can see that you have a genuine difficulty and are being honest with them, they will probably accept a fair compromise and not worry too much about it. But if they think you are trying to hoodwink them they will probably look elsewhere next time.

Of course you also must be sensitive to their needs and judge how important your commitment is to them. The Head Parkkeeper will probably not worry too much if you are going to be a couple of days late delivering a load of topsoil – but the bride-to-be will not be so forgiving about a long delay in producing her wedding dress!

3. YOU HAVE BEEN RUN OVER BY A BUS!

The only acceptable reason for neither delivering on time or contacting the other person to renegotiate is if you are seriously incapacitated – by accident, illness or emergency. In this situation – if you are capable of doing it – you will obviously have to rethink your priority list pretty urgently, and any business commitments are likely to come much further down the list than domestic and family considerations.

If you can't fulfil your commitment because you have been let down by a third party – because vital parts were not available, or the baby-sitter didn't turn up – then again, you are clearly not to blame and couldn't have foreseen the problem.

Being incapacitated through illness, accident or disaster will generate sympathy, but the job will still not have been done. All you can do is try to ensure that alternative arrangements are put in place as soon as possible – and all you can expect are a few Brownie Points, at best, for being as helpful as you can. And be aware: however much people may accept that you have failed to deliver for reasons completely outside your control, your are unlikely to get away with it more than once. If you start to get a reputation for unreliability – for whatever reason – it is very hard to make up lost ground.

DELIVERING ON YOUR COMMITMENTS

As you know by now, the **TRIM** course is built on the idea that by keeping your promises and doing the right thing, you will become a valued colleague, friend and family member. So it is no surprise that **TRIM's** emphasis is on delivering on your commitments. How can you make sure that you always come up with the goods, rather than negotiating a price for failure? How can you make promises with confidence? How do you know you are going to be able to deliver without having to renegotiate?

The first principle is not to over-promise. You should only ever make commitments in areas where you know you have the ability to do what you say you can. Don't offer to carry out brain surgery unless you are a brain surgeon.

If you are asked to carry out something you know is beyond your capabilities, say so – it sounds simple, but you would be surprised how many people seem to be unable to admit that some jobs are outside their own field of expertise.

Secondly, only promise to deliver to a timescale that you know you can meet – preferably, set it yourself. Often you will be pressed to deliver earlier: don't give in unless you're sure you can! Only you are aware of the other commitments you have, as well as potential delays from others who might need to be involved.

Finally, when you have made a promise – record it. We will look later at the various ways you might use to record your commitments and allocate time to them.

SOME MORE PRIORITY SETTING TIPS

When you are looking at a pile of jobs ahead of you, you can get them roughly in the order that will work best for you by using one of the three systems we discussed at the beginning of this chapter. Then, and as your day progresses, you can make sure that the order is still right by applying the 'kicking' test. All of this should keep you usefully employed on the tasks that are most important to you!

However, there are one or two other factors that you will also want to take into consideration when you're deciding what to do next.

Time

How much do you have? Your Terrain Map will tell you where is your next **Place to Be**, and when you have to be there. What job can you fit into the available time-slot, or at least make a worthwhile start on?

Deadlines

Does any of your tasks have a looming deadline that means you need to work on it straight away?

Negotiation

Do you know that you are going to fail to meet a commitment? If so, now is the time to call the other person and negotiate your way out of the problem. However, there are obvious constraints: if you know the person is just about to leave for a meeting, or in the middle of lunch, they will be in a better mood to talk if you call them later!

Personal preferences

What would *you* like to do now? You will probably make a better job of something you actually enjoy doing than something you detest. Sounds like procrastination? Well, maybe it is – but if you have a choice, give yourself a break and do what you like. Tomorrow you'll be less tired and better able to deal with the horrors!

Two-minute specials

Some tasks are inevitably going to fall into the category of 'Urgent but not Important'. Very often, the easiest way to get rid of them is simply to do them – then you have the satisfaction of ticking them off, and you don't need to bother with them again. This can be a quick way of tidying up your list without wasting valuable time. A good rule of thumb is that if you can finish a task in less than two minutes, you can deal with it without interrupting your 'proper' jobs.

Everything that you do in the **TRIM** course – all of the tools and techniques – rely to some extent on your ability to prioritise. You need to be able to decide what you're going to do next. Most people do this intuitively, on autopilot. If you spend a little time each day thinking about it rationally, you will be well ahead of the game.

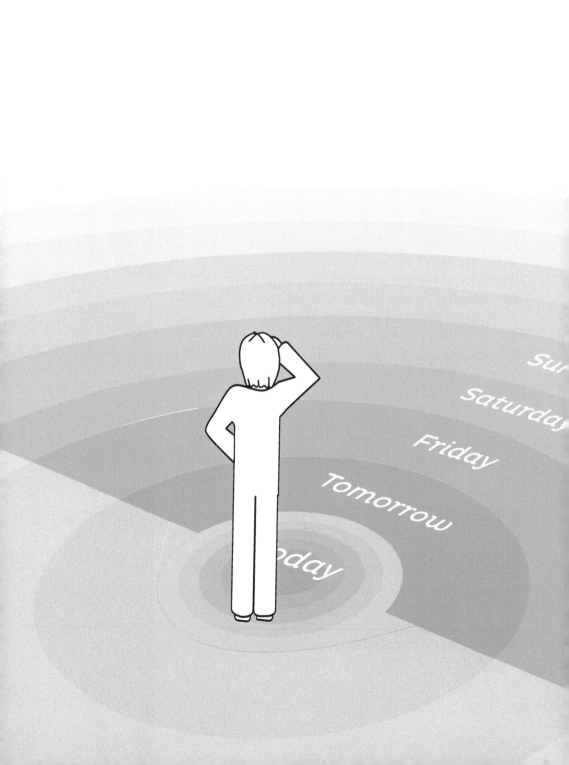

Terrain Maps

Putting you on the map

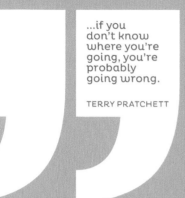

...if you
don't know
where you're
going, you're
probably
going wrong.

TERRY PRATCHETT

PUTTING YOU ON THE MAP

Or, more accurately, showing you where you are on the map – and where you're going. **TRIM's** Terrain Map gives you an exact picture of where you want to be, and what you would like to be doing, throughout your day – but because you are making the map, deciding what it shows and what the colours should be, you become the centre of your world. Everything revolves around you!

The point of a map, of course, is not only to show you where you are, but to remind you of the right route to follow to arrive where you want to be. Your Terrain Map does exactly this – but for your day, not for the ground beneath your feet. It will tell you what you plan to be doing at any given moment, what comes next and what you should already have achieved – and if things are going a bit off track, what you can do to recover the situation.

Here's the scheme. About a week in advance, as part of the **Weekly Helicopter Trip** you'll find out about in a couple of chapters, you work out the places you will need to be, things you will need to do and people you will be dealing with in the coming week – in other words, you draw up a plan. Your Terrain Map is where you set it all out, to make sure that everything fits realistically into your day with no dramatic overlaps or duplications – and where you will work out how to deal with all the developments (welcome and unwelcome!) which are bound to creep up on you – the 'Incoming Fire'.

As the day progresses, you will constantly be consulting your Terrain Map to check on progress, make sure that you are moving efficiently from place to place and task to task, and decide how best to react when things are not going according to your plan.

The Terrain Map is the first of the main **TRIM** tools. It's where you bring together all the various elements of action and information which are created by your interactions, and which will make sure that future interactions turn out as you want them to. **TRIM** has been developed to help make you are as effective, reliable and successful as possible. Terrain Maps are what makes the whole system work for you.

SO WHAT IS A TERRAIN MAP, ANYWAY...?

It is simply a way of laying out, in the way that suits you best, where you should be, what you should be doing and who you should be interacting with at any given moment.

It's not:
- ☒ a diary
- ☒ a to-do list
- ☒ a contact list.

Instead it takes elements of all three of these (and draws on them) to produce something much more valuable which helps you to arrange things most effectively, and see at a glance what you should be concentrating on at any given moment. *This will be the single most important thing in the world to you at that point in time.*

This is a really important point so let me explain it. Maybe you go to work every morning. Unless you are very lucky and love your job, you would probably prefer to be doing something else – playing football, meeting friends, watching TV or whatever. But you choose to go to work because that's how you make the money to do the things you actually enjoy.

In the same way, you might decide to spend more time writing a report than you absolutely need to: you could get away with producing a less well-researched paper, but you put the extra effort in because (as well as your natural pride in doing a good job!) it may help you towards promotion or a bonus.

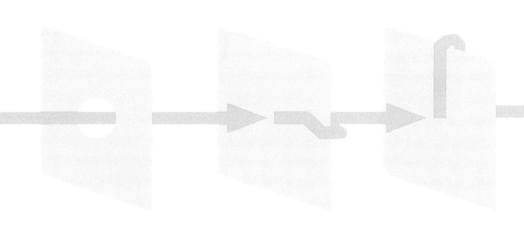

We all spend time on activities that we wouldn't necessarily choose for ourselves, but the vital point is that we decide to do so because that is the best way to move towards achieving our overall goals. Of course, we don't laboriously sit and decide on every action – but we know that if we just gave up our job, or performed badly at it, that would wreck our chances of buying a new car, or taking a dream holiday, or whatever else we have set as our goals.

Once we have made that judgment, we can be satisfied that even if we don't like what we're doing, we are still doing it because we know it's the very best option for us. So there's no point in worrying about it or complaining – we are working for our own best interests. At that moment, there is nothing else that we

could be doing which would be more important for our long-term happiness.

So – back to our Terrain Map. Think about the information you use to manage your day successfully.

For any given moment you need to know:
➜ where you should be
➜ where you are going next
➜ what you should be doing
➜ who you should be interacting with

As well as your immediate activities, you will have a whole range of other actions to fit in around them - phone calls to make, emails to read and send, projects to work on, and personal things like meeting friends, picking up the kids, and buying stuff for dinner.

Your Terrain Map is the place where all this information will be constantly available to guide you. So what does it look like?

Let's get started.

GOAL!

There are examples and templates for **Terrain Maps** in Chapter 6 (which will give examples and exercises for **Terrain Map** use), but let's begin by designing your own from first principles. In this exercise don't worry about where the actual information will come from - we'll deal with that later. Just put down what you think would be valuable for you to have at your fingertips as you go through the day.

Start off with a blank A4 piece of paper, in portrait form (with the long side up-and-down). When you start doing this for real you may well choose to use a completely different size or format, or a notebook, or just a laptop screen or even a smartphone. We will look at some of the advantages and disadvantages of all these – but there's plenty of time to refine your technique later! Put the date and day at the top of the page – you will end up with a few of these **Maps**.

PLACES TO BE

Begin by thinking about '**Places to Be**'. The size and importance of this bit of the page varies enormously from person to person, and from day to day. If you have a job which keeps you in one place – an office, shop or factory – then that will be your **Place to Be** for most of the working day (though of course you may need to move around your workplace for meetings, deliveries or whatever). But life isn't that simple! Life goes on (or maybe even begins!) after working hours. You might need to remember that you're due to play football every Thursday evening, or that you're meeting a friend off the 18.25 train on Tuesday, or that you have a doctor's appointment after work on Wednesday.

On the other hand, maybe you have a job that involves a constant round of travels and meetings. In this case you will certainly need always to know just where you're supposed to be, who you're seeing and where you need to travel to next.

Either way, the place where you physically have to be will define what else you can (or can't!) do. If you have a meeting in Birmingham all morning, you are not going to be able to meet your best friend for lunch in Manchester! So your list of **Places to Be** through the day is the most important part of the Terrain Map. Start off at the top left of the page and leave a good margin for notes you may want to make later.

You don't have to be precise, writing addresses and so on – just whatever you need to make things clear for you. So 'school', 'Burrows & Co', 'Mum's' are all fine. The exception is, of course, when you are going somewhere you have never been before and might need to remind yourself of the exact address, maybe with a postcode for your Satnav. Sometimes you might also want to jot down a phone number for your contact so you can get in touch if plans change – though of course if you are using a laptop or smartphone you may already have easy access to this kind of background information.

At this stage you need to make quite an important decision. When you put down the time of a **Place to Be** does this mean the time you actually have to be there, or the time you need to leave the last place to arrive in time for your activity? If you have an appointment with the dentist at 11.30, do you note down 11.30 – or 10.45, when you will have to leave home to catch the bus? Either of

these is perfectly valid – but you must be consistent! Personally I put in the travel time separately, so that I always know just where I'm supposed to be.

If my travel involves a rail journey or flight, I often jot down times of departures and arrivals so that it's easier to plan other events around them – it also saves scrabbling around for my ticket or boarding passes to confirm details!

Sometimes you might find that you have too many notes, and the Terrain Map itself is starting to get a bit 'overloaded'. It should always be simple and clear, so that you can get an instant snapshot of what's going on – you don't want to have to wade through all sorts of related notes which complicate the picture. If this starts to happen, just start a separate sheet, which you can attach to the back of the Terrain Map itself.

THINGS TO DO

When you are happy that you have listed all of your **Places to Be**, you can move on to **Things to Do**. Start a new list, at the top right of the page.

Here you are going to put down all of the Things you need to Do – yes, the clue is in the title – in rough order. But what order? You have two options: listing in order of importance, or listing in the order that you expect to actually do them in. Your list will contain both the jobs you need to get done, and the people you need to contact separately.

If you are a fan of Time Management books, you will already know that the tasks that appear most urgent are often not the most important ones – and that some really vital activities can actually be left until later. To put it another way: at some stage you have to renew your car insurance – the consequences of not doing so could be catastrophic. But you don't need to do it till next week, so it is important but not yet urgent. We will look at this perplexing problem later: but for now, all you need to know is that the **Things to Do** that you put on your Terrain Map should be only the ones that you intend to tackle on the day that you are planning. You would only put 'renew car insurance' on your Terrain Map if you had decided that you actually wanted to do it today.

Your **Things to Do** list is not a 'Task List'. Task Lists are very often a 'brain dump' of everything people can think of that they have to accomplish – ever! Some systems sort them into 'most urgent first' or 'most important'. But the almost inevitable outcome is that it's impossible to accomplish everything on the list – and so you lose heart, lose interest and eventually lose the list! In contrast, your Terrain Map **Things to Do** list should contain only what you can realistically achieve during that day. It shouldn't be either a 'wish-list' or a 'challenge'.

If you know that you need to write an essay, or clean out a cupboard, or prepare a project plan, or anything else that you won't have time to complete in one go – simply put it down as something to make a start on.

How much detail do you put in your '**Things to Do**'? Remember that these are simply aides-memoire! The entries in the list are not supposed to give you the complete background to projects, or all the points you want to make at a meeting. They may point you to where the information you need is stored, or even have a couple of key words – but you don't have room on your Terrain Map for loads of detail. Keep it simple!

Depending on how you spend your days, '**Things to Do**' might be a rich mixture of meetings to attend, phonecalls to make, emails to send, domestic chores to complete, items to dispatch, travel tickets to book…. As with everything in **TRIM**, you can adapt it as much as you like to fit your own lifestyle and work pattern. If some of them have to be completed by a specific time – mark that in. Highlight it or mark it up in red if it's really critical! What's important is that you should be able to look at your Terrain Map and see immediately where you are supposed to be and what you're supposed to be doing now – and how long until your next '**Place to Be**' (or until your next '**Thing to Do**' needs to be a 'thing done'!). There are examples at the end of this chapter.

So what happens when you become overwhelmed by unexpected developments – 'Incoming Fire'? Don't worry – this happens to everyone sometimes, and you can cope with it without feeling guilty about the things you didn't achieve. You'll see how later in in Chapter 6 (which gives examples and exercises for Terrain Map use).

KEY PEOPLE

Your **Things to Do** list will contain names of all sorts of contacts you need to phone, email or speak to during the day. However, you will probably find that there are a few – a very few – individuals you'll meet or talk to many times during the day, or who are specially important to you. These are your **Key People** – and with them, you will want to have some information instantly available, without having to refer to **People Folders**.

Just below your **Things to Do** list, start a section for these **Key People** you are going to interact with by meeting them, talking on the phone or messaging. This is not the place to put long notes about them – these should be in your separate **People Folders**, and that's where you may want to check whether there is particular information that you should remember about them. If there is, then write it down on your Terrain Map as 'trigger words' that will remind you of the key facts. Have they been ill/become grandparents/been promoted/won the lottery? Remember that you will make a far better impression if you are able to show that you care about them as people.

The main purpose of listing people you expect to interact with is to bring them to your mind and prompt you to look them up in your **People Folders**. However, you may also like to leave a bit of space around your list where you can make quick notes to remind you to update your **People Folders** later. (We'll talk in a later chapter about the best ways of 'capturing' interactions.)

PRIVATE

At the bottom right of your page, write down any private engagements or events you need to remember from when you leave work or have some free time. Apart from anything else, this might be a useful morale-booster and give you something to look forward to during the day!

Most of us also tend to remember the really important thing we had to buy, about five minutes after leaving the shop we could have bought it in! Write it down in the bottom right hand corner of your Terrain Map!

MEANWHILE, BACK IN THE REAL WORLD....

So – now you have a piece of A4 paper, with sections on **Places to Be**, **Things to Do**, **Key People**, and Private. This should give you all the information you need to make sure that you can run your day efficiently, keeping all your promises and delivering on your commitments – without stress or hassle. Can it really be that simple….?

Well, in an ideal world it might be. But in the world we actually live in, of course there are a few slight complications. Fortunately, your Terrain Map is designed to help you cope with them.

The main problem, of course, is that while the Terrain Map takes account of all the **Places to Be**, **Things to Do** and so on that you knew about when you put it together, our real-life circumstances are dynamic and always changing. As your day goes on, you will have countless interactions - events, phone calls, chance meetings, sudden revelations – that make life interesting but complicated! Some of this 'Incoming Fire' may be inconvenient or annoying – your commuter train is late, and when you arrive at your desk a message on your phone summons you to an urgent meeting in an hour's time. But other events will be welcome – in the conference room you come across an old friend from years back, and agree to meet for a drink after work; and as you munch your sandwich at lunchtime it dawns on you that since the IT guy from Head Office is here today, it's the perfect time to upgrade your computer. How is your carefully planned day looking now?

The ideal answer is – pretty good, really, but a bit different! Because you had your Terrain Map with you all day, you were able to make a couple of phonecalls from the train which you would normally have made from your desk. Later you were able to re-arrange an interview with a colleague to accommodate the meeting you were called to – and to ask a neighbour to pick up your son from his judo class while you're meeting your old friend for drinks. You know that you can cope with the computer being out of action for an hour by doing some background reading and writing today's report tomorrow instead. Phew!

What does look a bit battered, though, is your Terrain Map. As things happen and you adapt your plans, you will want to cross things off and write in the new **Places to Be** and **Things to Do**. Your Terrain Map is not about being neat and pretty – it is all about efficiency. By the end of the day, your A4 sheet may be a mass of scribbles and scorings-out – but you will still know just where you are supposed to be and what you should be doing.

What about these **Things to Do** that are now, quite clearly, not going to be done? If your Terrain Map was a 'Task List', they would all simply stay there and make you feel guilty: *Tasks Unaccomplished*. However, with a Terrain Map you are making decisions all the time – including those on what should be done now, and what should be postponed until another day. This 'culling' of tasks throughout the day – of crossing them off today's Terrain Map and transferring them to another day – is a demonstration that you are in control, and you have decided that there are more important things to do in the remaining part of the day. Oddly, this is a rewarding and liberating action – completely unlike the final task on the 'Task List', which consists of crossing off all the things that did not get done, and re-writing them onto tomorrow's Task List. What a negative way to finish off your day!

HOW TO FILL IN THE TERRAIN MAP

So far we have just used a made-up
Terrain Map as an example. How is a
real Terrain Map constructed?

Obviously, the basic things you have to
know are where you will need to be, what
you will need to do, and who are the
people with whom you will be interacting.
You'll get this information from a variety
of sources: **Diaries**, **Subject Folders**,
People Folders – and your own head.

In Chapter 7 we will look at the second
main **TRIM** tool – the **Weekly Helicopter
Trip**. This is a process which brings
together the inputs from all these various
sources and enables you to look ahead to
plan your activities for the next few days.
At this stage you will start to formulate
Terrain Maps for the days ahead, and
then as these days approach you will be
able to fill in more and more detail until
you should have a complete picture at the
start of each day.

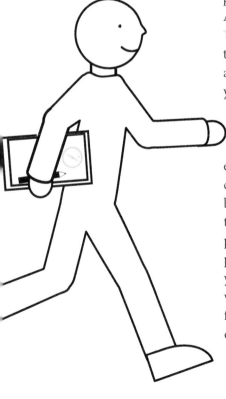

There are plenty, case studies and
examples which will increase your
confidence and ability throughout the
book. But I can't emphasise too strongly
that Terrain Maps are the ultimate
personal tool – although the basic
principles remain the same throughout,
you are the only person who can know
what format and content work best
for you. Believe me – when you have
developed your own personalized edition,
it will fit you like a glove and you'll never
want to be without it!

VARIANTS

The Terrain Map we have made up and used as an example is only one way of achieving the same result. As always, there are numerous other ways of doing it, including many digital solutions. Microsoft Outlook, in conjunction with OneNote, can produce a very sophisticated variation. (Chapter 10 looks at this whole area in more detail.)

I am a great fan of tablet and smartphone based variations of most parts of the **TRIM** system because they cut down dramatically on the number of separate bits of paper needed to maintain diaries, people and project folders. However, after trying a number of ideas for digital versions of the Terrain Map, I really believe that for this particular **TRIM** tool, 'paper is best'. You can't scribble or scratch out on a screen, and smartphones are just too small to give me the kind of overview of my day that I need from my Terrain Map. Maybe you can get a tablet to behave better than I can, but I still find that when I'm trying to make quick amendments, additions or strikethroughs on a complicated page, something always goes wrong and I end up spending more time than I save.

Of course, you may be completely at home with electronics, and think that it's crazy to rely on making dirty marks on clean bits of paper to navigate around your day! If so, that's fine and you will probably be able to design a fully-integrated daily management system that you're completely comfortable with – though I bet that at the end of the day you can't crumple it up into a ball for the cat to play with. We'll look again at electronics and **TRIM** in Chapter 10.

HOW TO USE YOUR TERRAIN MAP

I hope that you've now firmly got the idea that your Terrain Map is there for you, not for anyone else. The way you lay it out (and use it) is entirely up to you.

Remember that the only reason you are going through this exercise, of preparing, updating and consulting your Terrain Map, is to make it easier for you to run your day in the most effective way possible. 'Effective' doesn't mean 'effective for someone else' – that's part of the story and it may be what you are trying to achieve (because, ultimately, that suits you best!) But in this context 'effective' means with most benefit and least hassle for you. So everything you do with your Terrain Map is intended to be directly helpful for you.

TOP SECRET

The Undercover Operator

There may be times when it is inconvenient or inappropriate to be seen consulting a **Terrain Map** (or even worse, **People Folders** or **Subject Folders**!) in a meeting. In a later chapter we will look at **TRIM** tools to remain efficient and effective in these situations.

Adapt, adapt, adapt

Try different ways of setting out your Terrain Maps
– size of paper, using a notebook, using a desk diary,
keeping it all on your laptop. All these techniques
have advantages and disadvantages – see which one
works best for you.

Be messy
As long as you can understand what's on your
Terrain Map, that's all that matters. So if it ends
up – or even starts the day – a mass of crossings out,
lines and arrows, that's fine. If that is the way it suits
you to do it – you're the boss!

Be colourful
You might find it useful to differentiate your
Things to Do and **Places to Be** by entering them in
different colours. Or make personal plans, or project
meetings, or specially important items, stand out in
red. Or use blue paper for your Terrain Map so you
can always find it instantly among your other papers.

Be personal
It's your bit of paper – and unless you drop it in
the corridor, no-one else is going to see it. Put
on it whatever suits you, be honest and be direct.
There's no point in filling it in for other people -
unless you're a dedicated diarist, it's about the most
personal item you'll create.

Experiment
What have you got to lose? Once you get used to
them, you'll find it hard to do without your Terrain
Maps and you'll use them every day - so you might
as well get them into the format and style that's
going to work best for you. The only way to do this
is to keep trying new ideas till you feel everything is
just right – and even then you'll probably find there's
room for improvement. I still do all of the time!

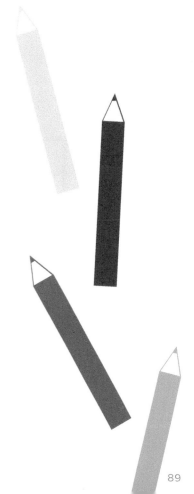

Using your Terrain Map

Practice navigation

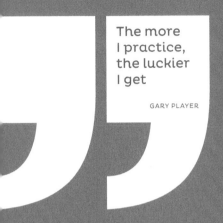

> **The more I practice, the luckier I get**
>
> GARY PLAYER

This chapter will give you a better idea of how Terrain Maps work in the real world, and show you some examples of different ways of setting them out and using them. At the end, you can have a go at making up your own Terrain Map for what you expect to do tomorrow.

Finally, you will see how much easier it is to create your Terrain Maps using another of the main **TRIM** tools – the **Weekly Helicopter Trip**, which we'll be covering in the next chapter.

If you're quite happy that you understand Terrain Maps and just want to get on with the **TRIM** course, feel free to skip this chapter. You can always come back to it later.

A DAY IN THE LIFE

TIM'S DAY

KATHY'S DAY

MAKE YOUR OWN....

EXAMPLES OF
TERRAIN MAP

A DAY IN THE LIFE

I'll start off by looking at how a couple using their Terrain Maps might handle a typical day. I've chosen Kathy, who runs her own conference planning business from home. She's married to Tim, who works in a medium-sized business. Tim is working on a couple of projects and is trying to persuade another company to collaborate in one of them. Kathy and Tim's daughter Madge is in primary school.

It's Thursday 15 November.

Tim has a tough day ahead in the office, and Kathy will be out and about seeing customers and inspecting venues.

TIM'S DAY

LET'S LOOK AT TIM'S DAY FIRST.
Here are the '**Places to Be**' from his diary:

9.00 – 10.00   MANAGEMENT MEETING BOARD ROOM

11.00 – 12.00   PROJECT ALBA STATUS CONF. 1

14.00 – 16.00   PERSONAL DEVELOPMENT PLAN ASSESSMENTS
MEETING ROOM
14.00 Dave Brown
14.30 Janet Robinson
15.00 Claire Arbuthnot
15.30 Brian Mercier

16.30   COLLECT MADGE AFTER SCHOOL CLUB

19.00   ERIC'S LEAVING PARTY CONF. 1

And here are his '**Things to Do**':

RETURN TELEPHONE CALLS TO:
Mike
Louise
Mary T
John Attridge
Guy Smith
Seb Cohen
Mary Groves

PHONE (NEW CALLS)
Market Research - for Project Pluto Feedback
Alistair Deal
Jonathan Brown
Gail Davidson
Amanda Turner

SPEAK TO (COLLEAGUES IN OFFICE)
Jason Q
Belinda
Accounts

WORK ON
Regional Expansion Plans
Own PDP
Staff Christmas Party
New staff appointment letters

TIM ALSO HAS A FEW PERSONAL ITEMS TO ATTEND TO:
Buy Earl Grey tea bags
Buy 2 light bulbs
Write job application letters

PHEW! QUITE A DAY. LET'S SEE WHAT TIM'S TERRAIN MAP LOOKS LIKE.

Thursday 15 November

Places to Be

9.00 – 10.00   Management Meeting
                  – Board Room

11.00 – 12.00   Project Alba – status
                  – conf. 1

14.00 – 16.00   Personal Dev. Plans
                  – Meeting Room
        14.00 – Dave Brown
        14.30 – Janet Robinson
        15.00 – Claire Arbuthnot
        15.30 – Brian Menier

16.30   –   collect Madge from A/S Club
                  (back to office after?)

19.00   –   Eric's leaving party
                  – Conf. 1

Key Contact

Barry Evans (wife broken leg?)
Janet Robinson (cat health?)

Things to Do

Return phonecalls:
        Mike
        Louise
        Mary T
        John Attridge
        Debbie Smith
        Seb Cohen
        Mary Groves

Phone:
        Market Research
        (for Project Pluto Feedback)
        Alistair Deal
        Jonathan Brown
        Gail Davidson
        Amanda Turner

Speak to:
        Jason Q
        Belinda
        Accounts

Work on
Regional Expansion Plans
Own PDP
Staff Christmas Party
New staff appointment letters

Personal
        Buy Earl Grey Teabags, lights
        write job application letters

So – there's the plan. We've seen what Tim had in his diary for **Places to Be** and **Things to Do**, and he has incorporated them all into the Terrain Map that is going to help him navigate his way through the day.

Now let's see how it all actually pans out – and what his **Terrain Map** looks like afterwards!

Here's how Thursday 15 November progresses for Tim, and how he reacts as his plans and priorities are buffeted by the avalanche of events.

Tim's actions are in red.

THURSDAY 15 NOVEMBER

8.30

Mail arrives
· Invoice for Project Alba Good, I'll take that to the meeting
· Mailshot about office furniture Bin
· Status reports from South on Project Neptune Put in Neptune stack on desk

E-mails
· Brian Toms - "Yes to North. Details Please" Move to 'Action' folder
· Jane Ellis – "Family emergency – won't make Project Alba meeting before 11.30"
  Jane is key player, essential for meeting – ask Philip to speak to others involved
  and delay start of meeting for 30 minutes.
· + 11 spam or irrelevant Delete

Voicemails
· Terry Jones – "Please call re your proposal" Put on Terrain Map, high priority
· Debbie Smith returning call from 3 days ago Put on Terrain Map
· Brian Toms – "Please call re North trip" Put on Terrain Map

8.40

Incoming call
· Barry Evans (Tim's boss)
    · Confirm Agenda for 0900 management meeting? Yes, or he'd have been told.
    · Update on Project Alba meeting – why did Tim have to reschedule?
    One-minute rundown, discuss any necessary action before rescheduled meeting.
    · Nag about PDPs – staff this pm and own for Monday? Yes, all in hand
    (Call ends 0850)

10.20

Return from Management Meeting
20 minutes late as usual! Record actions, new tasks, information
E-mails:
· all spam Bin
Voicemail:
· call Kathy at home before 10.30
Too late – add to Terrain Map

10.30 – 11.00

Gets on with phonecalls to Terry Jones, Mike, Louise, John Attridge.
Speaks to Jason, Belinda. Record resulting actions, information

11.00 – 11.25

Uses 'gift of time' from 30-minute postponement of Alba meeting to
work on his own PDP.

11.25

Incoming call Leave to go to voicemail, too close to 11.30 meeting

12.30

Return from Project Alba meeting Record actions, new tasks, information
E-mails:
· Brian Toms –" Thanks for North details" File
· Yvonne Coultard – "More details about South please"
  Ask Philip to send
· 3 spam Bin
Voicemail:
· Kathy – "in taxi. Please call – urgent" Call. Confirm picking up Madge.
· 'Competitions Ltd' – "Please call re training course"
  Put on Terrain Map for tomorrow
· Brian – "Can't make 15.30 – please call" Call. Reschedule for tomorrow
  17.30 – on Terrain Map and in Places to Be Diary – to avoid double booking.
In-tray:
· Brochure copy first draft with visuals.
  Needs input/approval within 2 days Onto Reading Stack
· Invitation to Chambers Network Event Onto Reading Stack

12.45

Sally and Brian ask to talk to Tim – 'problems with Samantha' Meet in office

Thursday 15 November

Places to Be

9.00 - 10.00   Management Meeting
                - Board Room

11.00 - 12.00   Project Alba - status
11.30 - 12.30   - conf. 1

14.00 - 16.00   Personal Dev. Plans
                - Meeting Room
        14.00 - Dave Brown
        14.30 - Janet Robinson
        15.00 - Claire Arbuthnot   -talk to Brian
        15.30 - Brian Menier   Nov 17.30 tomorrow

16.30   -   collect Madge from A/S Club
              (back to office after?)
                          Yes!

19.00   -   Eric's leaving party
              - Conf. 1

Key Contact

Barry Evans (wife broken leg?)
Janet Robinson (cat health?)

Kathy: call urgent

Things to Do

Return phonecalls:
    Mike
    Louise   Brian Toms
    Mary T   re North
    John Attridge
    Debbie Smith tomorrow
    Seb Cohen
    Mary Groves

Phone: 447.2392
                        Terry Jones*
    Market Research
    (for Project Pluto Feedback)
    Alistair Deal
    Jonathan Brown
    Gail Davidson
    Amanda Turner
    Kathy
        CompetitionsLtd
Speak to:
    Jason Q
    Belinda
    Accounts

Work on
Regional Expansion Plans
Own PDP
Staff Christmas Party
New staff appointment letters

Personal
    Buy Earl Grey Teabags, lights
    write job application letters

13.00

Gerald Tenon arrives unexpectedly. Needs to talk about North
Have lunch with him – easiest way of dealing with this quickly. Take all
relevant Information, Subject & People specific, to the lunch meeting.

13.45

Return from lunch Record actions, new tasks, information

13.55

Incoming call Leave to go to voicemail, too close to 14.00 PDP meeting

15.30

PDP Assessments finished Record actions, new tasks, information

Uses 'gift of time' from postponing Brian's PDP interview to tackle:
E-mails:
· Spam x 3 Delete
· Garth Rabbitt – "Can we meet for lunch in the next 2 weeks?"
  2 minute reply suggesting next Thursday – note in Places to Be diary.
Voicemails:
· Gail Davidson and Amanda Turner returned calls
  Put on Terrain Map
· Gillian Green returned call re Project Pluto. Put on Terrain Map
· Barry Evans – "Please call asap" Call now
  Record actions, new tasks, information

... AND THEN ON TO FINISH WORK ON REGIONAL EXPANSION PLAN

15.45

Incoming call
Sheena Bradley to discuss Project South
(Call ends 16.00 – record actions, new tasks, information)

Thursday 15 November

Places to Be

| 9.00 – 10.00 | Management Meeting |
| | – Board Room |

| ~~11.00 – 12.00~~ | Project Alba – status |
| 11.30 – 12.30 | – conf. 1 |

14.00 – 16.00	Personal Dev. Plans
	– Meeting Room
14.00 –	~~Dave Brown~~
14.30 –	~~Janet Robinson~~
15.00 –	~~Claire Arbuthnot~~ -talk to Brian
~~15.30 – Brian Menier~~	Nov 17.30 tomorrow

16.30 –	collect Madge ~~from~~ A/S Club
	(back to office after?)
	Yes!

| 19.00 – | Eric's leaving party |
| | – Conf. 1 |

Key Contact   No-only bad sprain

Barry Evans (wife broken leg?)

Janet Robinson (cat health?)
                Now OK

Kathy: call urgent

Things to Do

Return phonecalls:

~~Mike~~

~~Louise~~   Brian Toms

Mary T   re North

~~John Attridge~~

Debbie Smith tomorrow

~~Seb Cohen~~

Mary Groves

Phone:
                        447.2392
                    Terry Jones*

~~Market Research~~

(for ~~Project~~ Pluto Feedback)

~~Alistair~~ Deal

~~Jonathan Brown~~

Gail Davidson -tomorrow

Amanda Turner -tomorrow

Kathy
    CompetitionsLtd

Speak to:

~~Jason Q~~

~~Belinda~~

~~Accounts~~

Work on

~~Regional Expansion Plans~~

~~Own PDP~~

~~Staff Christmas Party~~

New staff ~~appointment~~ letters

Personal

Buy Earl Grey Teabags, lights

write job application letters

16.00 - 16.45

- Phones Market Research for Project Pluto feedback
  Record information
- Phones Alistair Deal, Jonathan Brown Records information
- Phones Accounts

16.15 - 17.00

Taking Madge from school to friend's house

17.00

Back at office after collecting Madge
Voicemail
Sally Jones – 'Please call – urgent' Call now. Personnel problem.
Record actions, new tasks, information

17.15

- Brian asks to speak to Tim. Follow-up on Samantha. Record actions,
  new tasks, information.
- Drafts new staff appointment letter
- Puts sticky note on car keys reminding himself to buy teabags and
  lightbulbs on way home.

17.45

Tim's time is now his own! Except for Eric's leaving
party at 19.00... Should he leave and go home now
before returning for the Party? In fact, he decides to
be a good boy and stay at his desk catching up/getting
ahead on Action and/or Reading Stacks for the next
hour - so he is able to finish off the staff appointment
letters and make plans for the Office Christmas Party.
He makes sure that he puts his phone on divert to
voice mail, and ignores in-coming e-mails!)

So, by the end of the day Tim
has managed to complete
most of the **Things to Do** on
his **Terrain Map**. Those he
hasn't tackled – only a couple
of phone calls – he transfers
to tomorrow's **Terrain Map**
and scores off today's. What
a great feeling of satisfaction!
Even better if he'd transferred
it earlier on in the day...

KATHY'S DAY

Kathy uses her Terrain Map slightly differently.

Here's how her **Places to Be** diary looks:

08.30 – 0915: Madge to school
11.00 – 12.00: Venue visit – Albion Hotel
13.00 – 14.00: Lunch with George R - Vista Bistro
14.30 – 17.00: BBS Conference – Fountain Hall
19.00 – 20.00: Madge swimming class

And her 'office' **Things to Do**

PHONE:
George
Mike
Caroline Gray (Albion)
Vodafone re new mobile
Return calls to:
Rosemary Smith
Belinda Downs
Bill F

VAT return/accountant
Quotation for Higgs – AGM 24 January
Print name-badges for Tuesday

PLUS A FEW PERSONAL THINGS:
Take in Dry Cleaning
Pay TV Licence
Phone Madge's piano teacher
Call plumber

Another busy day!

Kathy organises her Terrain Map in a slightly different way.
Let's have a look:

15 November   Thursday   **Week 46**

8.00		
	School Run (see Meg)	
9.00		
10.00		
11.00	Look at Albion Hotel (esp. table numbers)	
12.00	← Bus 67	
13.00	George R lunch - Vista (is he bidding for RSA?)	
14.00	2.30 - 5	
15.00	RAS Conference - Fountain Hall (check numbers)	
16.00		
17.00		
18.00		
19.00	Madge swimming remember towel this time!!	

To do

Phone:
- George re lunch
- Mike re RSA bid
- Caroline Gray 543-2016 (before 10.30 re Albion job)
Voda phone - phone replacement.

Call back: 306-4271
- Rosie Smith (book group)
- Belinda Davies - party conference
- Bill F
_____

VAT Return /accountant
Quotation for Higgs
- AGM 24/1
Print name badges for Tues.

Evening

Personal
- Take in dry cleaning
- Pay TV licence
- Phone Madge piano teacher
     345 - 7295
- call plumber (again!!) 746- 0134

Remember
- Meg - holiday plan
- George - has Sue had baby

Kathy uses her page-a-day desk diary to give a more visual picture of her **Places to Be**, using the right-hand side of the page to list **Things to Do**. She also puts in a bit more detail than Tim, with key words to prompt her memory – or remind her to look at her project or people folders. She uses colours and highlights to emphasise the more important or time-sensitive tasks. One advantage of this method is that it makes it easier for Kathy to capture future **Places to Be**, and some **Things to Do**, in the same book. The disadvantage is that she needs to lug it around with her!

Let's have a look at how Kathy's day unfolds.

8.30

Kathy takes Madge to school – meets Meg, and remembers to ask about her holiday plans. Makes a quick note on her Terrain Map, to transfer when she gets home. On the way home, Kathy drops off the dry-cleaning.

She has highlighted her phonecalls to George (to confirm lunch), Caroline Gray (to confirm her 11.00 visit) and to Rosie Smith, so she makes these as soon as she gets into her home office.

Before leaving for her venue visit at the Albion Hotel, Kathy is able to complete her VAT return and file it online. As it's getting near the end of her financial year, she also calls her accountant and makes an appointment to see him the following week – noted to transfer later.

Sudden thought: she can't remember if Tim confirmed he was able to pick up Madge from after school club. She calls his office and leaves a voicemail.

10.30

Kathy sets out to walk to the Albion Hotel – she only notes times of actual appointments on her Terrain Map, not how long she'll spend travelling.

11.00 – 12.00

Venue visit at the Albion Hotel. Kathy needs to note prices, facilities and so on in some detail in her workbook, so doesn't need to make any extra entry on the Terrain Map.

8.00	
	School Run (see Meg)
9.00	Going on holiday to Malta mid Feb
10.00	
11.00 ↕	Look at Albion Hotel (esp. table numbers)
12.00	← Bus 67
13.00	George R lunch - Vista ⟨Now 1.15⟩ (is he bidding for RSA?) Yes!
14.00	
15.00 ↕	2.30 - 5 RAS Conference - Fountain Hall (check numbers)
16.00	
17.00	
18.00	
19.00 ↑	Madge swimming — remember towel this time!!
Evening	Personal

Personal
- Take in dry cleaning ✓
- Pay TV licence
- Phone Madge piano teacher 345 - 7295 ✓
- call plumber (again!!) 746- 0134
  left message - call again tomorrow

Remember
- Meg - holiday plan
- George - has Sue had baby

To do

Phone:
- George ✓ lunch 1.15
- Mike re RSA bid
- Caroline Gray 543-2016 ✓ (before 10.30 re Albion job)

Voda phone - phone replacement.

Call back: 306-4271
- Rosie Smith ✓ (book group)
- Belinda Davies - party conference
- Bill F

VAT Return /accountant ✓
Quotation for Higgs ⟨27 Nov 10.30⟩
- AGM 24/1
Print name badges for Tues.

After the visit, Kathy takes the number 67 bus across town for her lunch appointment with George. She calls Tim again to check about picking up Madge. On the way she has a quick mental rehearsal of the points she wants to get across: George's company may be bidding for a major contract with training firm RSA, and if so, Kathy would like to get the contract for arranging their conferences.

Because George asked if they could postpone lunch by 15 minutes she arrives at the restaurant a few minutes early and is able to make phone calls to Madge's piano teacher and Bill F, and to leave a message asking the plumber to call her back. Tim rings to confirm collecting Madge.

13.15 – 14.15

Lunch with George, who confirms he is bidding for the RSA contract. Kathy makes an initial pitch for providing conference organisation and they agree to meet again. Kathy makes notes in her workbook. George is pleasantly surprised when Kathy asks about Sue's baby.

14.15

Kathy has to take a taxi to the BBS Conference because lunch ran late – but she had factored this in after her early morning phonecall to George.

14.30 – 17.00

BBS Conference. Kathy is only there to check on arrangements and deal with any problems, so she has time to make phonecalls to Belinda and Vodafone, and even to make a good start on the Quotation for Higgs & Co's AGM on 24 January.

When Kathy gets home at half past five she can see that she has got through almost everything on the Terrain Map, except phoning Mike about the RSA bid and printing name badges for Tuesday – both of which she has already moved to tomorrow's Terrain Map. She has time to renew the TV Licence online – and to look out Madge's swimming towel for her lesson at seven o'clock.

Kathy's Terrain Map at the end of the day

8.00		To do
	School Run (see Meg)	
9.00	Going on holiday to Malta mid Feb	Phone:
10.00		- George re lunch 1.15 ✓
		- Mike re RSA bid tomorrow
11.00 ↕	Look at Albion Hotel (esp. table numbers)	- Caroline Gray 543-2016 (before 10.30 re Albion job)
12.00	← Bus 67	Voda phone - phone replacement. ✓
13.00	George R lunch - Vista 1.15 (Now) (is he bidding for RSA? Yes!	
14.00		Call back: 306-4271
15.00	2.30 - 5	- Rosie Smith (book group)
	RAS Conference - Fountain Hall (check numbers)	- Belinda Davies - party conference 24-25 Jan Feb ✓
16.00		- Bill F ✓
17.00	134 + 2 ?? - amend invoice	
18.00		VAT Return /accountant ✓ Quotation for Higgs 27 Nov 10.30 - AGM 24/1
19.00 ↑	Madge swimming remember towel this time!!	Print name badges for Tues.
Evening	Personal	Tomorrow!
	- Take in dry cleaning ✓	
	- Pay TV licence ✓	
	- Phone Madge piano teacher 345 - 7295	
	- call plumber (again!!) 746- 0134	
	left message - call again tomorrow	
	Remember	
	- Meg - holiday plan	
	- George - has Sue had baby	

Kathy's day has been a bit more predictable than Tim's. Throughout the day, she has always been able to check her Terrain Map both to ensure that she is where she is supposed to be, and to use free time between her **Places to Be** to tackle some of the tasks on her '**Things to Do**' list. All she needs to do now is to transfer a few items of information from today's Terrain Map to the appropriate folders, and then enjoy Madge's swimming lesson! Like Tim, she can also now score off everything on today's Terrain Map.

MAKE YOUR OWN....

You have seen how Tim and Kathy put together and use their Terrain Maps. Now have a go at making one up for yourself.

Choose a day when you know you'll have quite a bit on – childcare commitments, things to do around the house, meetings, classes or whatever. Tomorrow is ideal, because you probably have a very good idea of what will be going on and will be able to fill in plenty of detail.

Choose the layout and orientation of the page that you think will be best for you. If you think you're going to want to write notes about your '**Places to Be**' or '**Things to Do**', either before they happen or afterwards as a reminder of what you need to capture more permanently, you might find it easier to use a landscape format. On the other hand if you expect to have long lists of people to call, or appointments to attend, portrait could be better.

Start off as before, by listing your '**Places to Be**'. Have you decided whether you're going to include your travelling time to and from engagements? Remember, it doesn't matter whether you do or not – but you must be consistent! You may want to add a few notes about how you're going to travel, or a phone number for the person you're going to see, or a few words to remind you if you need to take something special to a meeting.

Then come your '**Things to Do**'. You might list them in order of priority, or if they are time-sensitive, in the order you will need to do them in. Be imaginative – use colours or even pictures to emphasise the most important tasks! Again, you might like to add a few notes – phone numbers or key facts about what you need to talk to people about.

If you expect to be interacting with people who are specially important to you, have a small section of the page for 'Key Contacts' where you can jot down some words to jog your memory about the significant things happening in their lives.

You will certainly have a few personal appointments or tasks that you want to get done during the day. Put them down in a separate area – maybe in a separate colour from your less attractive business-related jobs!

take notes!!

hints
tips
help your
memory

This is your Terrain Map in its most basic form – untested and untried by you, and made up on-the-fly in a few minutes! The next stage is – to use it. Take it with you on the day you've chosen, and see how well it actually reflects what happens to you throughout the day. If it's pretty accurate – great, then your system seems to work. If not, then you may need to rethink just what information you need through your day, and what you may need to add as events take place.

Either way, remember that your Terrain Map serves two purposes – not only to guide you through your activities and interactions, but to act as an *aide memoire* to make sure that you capture the information they produce and the actions you will need to take.

So – there you have it!

So far, we have only talked about creating Terrain Maps with information that you have in your head, or at best in your diaries, and just for tomorrow or a day in the very near future. In the next chapter I will introduce you to the next **TRIM** technique, which will let you fill in Terrain Maps for several days ahead, and keep updating them right up until the time comes to use them – making them a very powerful tool indeed.

EXAMPLES OF TERRAIN MAPS

The following pages contain examples of other possible templates of **Terrain Maps**. In a later chapter we'll look more closely at ways of keeping and using your **Terrain Map** in electronic form.

TRIM – TERRAIN MAP

DATE:

PLACES TO BE/THINGS TO DO

When   What   Where

PHONE CALLS

Who   When

KEY COLLEAGUES

KEY PERSONAL

PERSONAL/MISC

TRIM - TERRAIN MAP

DATE:

PLACES TO BE/THINGS TO DO

When	What	Where

PHONE CALLS

Who	When

KEY COLLEAGUES

KEY PERSONAL

PERSONAL/MISC

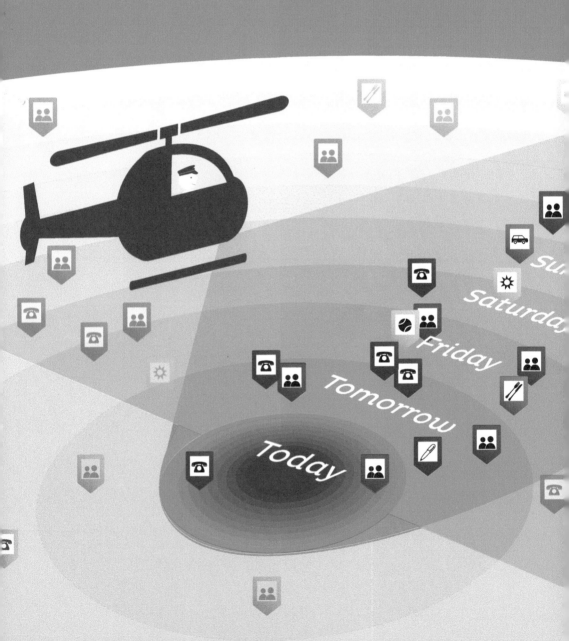

25 Minutes for a Better Week

The Weekly Helicopter Trip

I have a
cunning
plan...

BALDRIC

WHY PLAN?

Everyone plans. Each time you leave home, you have a plan: you're going to do something, see someone, go to the cinema, and you have in your head a pretty good idea of how you're going to do it – the route you'll take in the car, the bus you should catch, whether you will need to have cash available to buy a meal and so on.

So far so good. This kind of simple planning is fine for getting you from A to B, and maybe for the rough outline of what you'll do when you get there. But what it doesn't do is either help you to decide whether you should be making the trip in the first place, or work out what you're trying to achieve. Of course if your aim is two hours escape from reality in front of a cinema screen that's not a problem – but if you have a possibly difficult meeting, whether for business or with a family member or friend, some more detailed planning will stand you in good stead.

TRIM's main planning tool is the
Weekly Helicopter Trip – a regular review of
the past week's events and an initial planner for
the next two weeks. This helicopter view sets
everything in context and ensures no major
clashes: it gives you a real feeling of empowerment
when you know exactly where you plan to be and
what you will be able to achieve.

PLAN!

THE WEEKLY HELICOPTER TRIP WILL GIVE YOU
→ Forward planning
→ Terrain Mapping for up to 10 days in advance
→ Daily Action Sheets
→ 'Quiet time' for review, mental visualisation and
   mental rehearsals of the next two weeks events
→ Motivation for your long, medium and short-term goals

Of course innumerable things will happen in the
course of the time you're planning for, some of
them predictable (so plan!) and some right out of
the blue. But having an overall picture of the way
things should look is a great basis to work from!

EFFECTIVE FORWARD PLANNING

Planning does not mean writing down all the things that you would like to happen – that's called dreaming!

Real planning is about what you know is actually going to happen. Let's take a trivial example. Say you have an appointment with the dentist at 10am. You're going to travel by bus, the journey takes 15 minutes and buses go by every 15 minutes. How do you plan to arrive on time? The wishful thinker reckons he should be at the bus stop between 9.35 and 9.40 to have a good chance of a bus turning up in time. The punctilious patient gets there by 9.30 in case he just misses a bus and has to wait quarter of an hour. The **TRIM**–trained person, of course, checks the bus timetable and arrives at the stop a couple of minutes before the bus is due.

The point is that effective planning saves you time, gets you there on time and, by making sure that you don't waste other people's time, keeps them on your side.

The real value of planning is not simply that you are always in the right place, at the right time. That's important – and removes one of the main causes of stress in your own life – but the key point comes when you go beyond simple 'diary-planning' and begin to prepare yourself for what will happen when you arrive at your destination.

What will happen when you arrive at your destination?

As you know from Chapter 5, the things you need to plan for fall into two main categories – where you need to be, and what you need to do when you get there. Since you are following the **TRIM** system, you will already have a diary – or even two if you prefer – holding the outlines of **Places to Be** and **Things to Do**.

The other information that you will want to draw on for your **Helicopter Trip** is about the people who you will meet or talk to over the coming couple of weeks, and the subjects you will discuss or take action on. You should have that all stored in your **People Folders** and **Subject Folders** – whether these are physical, digital or just in your mind.

THE WEEKLY HELICOPTER TRIP

The **Weekly Helicopter Trip** is the tool that you will use to plan what's going to happen in the next fortnight. Your Terrain Map gives you the close-up view of the next 24 hours, complete with **Places to Be** and **Things to Do**. The **Weekly Helicopter Trip** takes you way up high so that you can see not only where you are now, but what the landscape looks like over the next fortnight. A nice, easy stroll through the meadows, with an occasional bridge to cross and pleasant people to lunch with? Or mountains to climb, rivers to ford and pitfalls to avoid at all costs? Whatever is coming up, it's best to be able to anticipate it and plan how to tackle it!

The **Weekly Helicopter Trip** should become part of your routine, so it's best to schedule it for a time when you are not likely to be run off your feet – so maybe not first thing Monday morning, when you may be dealing with the weekend's developments, or Friday afternoon when you probably want to think about starting the weekend. Of course, it may be that these are exactly the times that suit you best! If so, no problem – you're in charge! I always do it on a Wednesday morning. If you are able to do your planning at the same time every week, so much the better: but if you need to build in some flexibility that's fine, so long as you make sure that you do it regularly. *But if you need to move it, try to do it earlier, not later!* The **Helicopter Trip** is an essential element in your planning, and you should make it a high priority rather than putting it off.

25 minutes

Give yourself around half an hour and try to make sure that you won't be disturbed – you need space to think about this!

Don't try to squeeze your **Helicopter Trip** into 'existing' time – try to find extra time to do it by getting in to work a little early, or just deciding to make a short period every week completely unassailable. Give yourself around half an hour and try to make sure that you won't be disturbed – you need space to think about this!

You might find it useful to make up a template like the ones in Chapter 6 – but feel free to modify it as much as you like, so that it fits your situation and lets you put in all the information you need. If you're doing it electronically, try to do it on a desktop or laptop with a decent-sized screen. One of the main advantages is that you can see the whole two-week period at once, so you don't want to be scrolling round the window of a smartphone.

First make sure that your diary is absolutely up-to-date – check that everything in the old week can be completely crossed out, and anything that you had to move or repeat from last week is properly entered in your new diary. Then check for 'follow-ons'. Almost certainly some meetings, or phone calls, will have had knock-on effects which you'll already have factored in to your existing Terrain Maps and **Places to Be** and **Things to Do** diaries – but it's probably worth checking that you don't need to make any adjustments.

Now you can look ahead to the next fortnight. If you like to get everything down on paper, begin by printing off new Terrain Maps for the period from when your current Terrain Maps 'expire' – you will already have Terrain Maps for the next week

> Events,
> dear boy,
> events.
>
> HAROLD
> MACMILLAN

(from your last **Helicopter Trip**) so the new ones will be added on after them. If you prefer not to create actual Terrain Maps so far ahead, just use one or two pieces of paper – or their electronic equivalent. The most important thing is that you should end up with a visual representation of what you need to know about the places you will need to be, things you will have to do and people you will meet in the next fortnight.

At this stage you should be able to step back and take a look at the landscape for the next two weeks. How does it look? With the terrain mapped out in front of you, there should be no drastic clashes of appointments or impossible-to-fulfil commitments coming up – if there are, the system has gone wrong somewhere, but at least you should have time to rearrange things without too much hassle. This is the time to do it! You are in control of the next two weeks, as much as you ever can be, and nothing you can predict should take you unawares.

Your helicopter view will also highlight any gaps in your schedule which you might be able to put to good use – maybe to smooth out your workload, do some work on a pet project, or even take some time off!

Needless to say, in reality the next two weeks will come up with surprises which you will have to cope with. Every soldier knows that 'no plan survives first contact with the enemy', and the same is true of the beautiful Terrain Maps which emerge from your **Weekly Helicopter Trip**. You have already seen how battered and tattered each day's Terrain Map becomes as the day goes on, and the process is likely to start early! Unless you lead an unusually predictable life you are bound to have to remodel your plans to accommodate changes for all sorts of reasons:

"Events, dear boy, events", as British Prime Minister Harold Macmillan replied when asked what was his greatest challenge. But this is where the **Weekly Helicopter Trip** really proves its value. It gives you a full perspective of what's coming up, so that when you do have to make changes you know just where you have flexibility and where you may need to stand firm. It's much easier to fit things into a framework you know, than to simply chuck them into a random mix with who knows what knock-on effects!

When you are looking down from your helicopter at the next two weeks, what are the major features of the landscape you see – the mountains you may have to climb (or avoid), rivers you might have to cross? The chances are that your main obstacles will be **Places to Be**, **Things to Do** and **People** you will meet. We'll look briefly at each of these.

Up, up and away....

The **Weekly Helicopter Trip** doesn't just cover a single week – go higher and you see more!

Although normally you'll only want to review the past week, and see what will be coming up in the next two, you can look much further ahead if you want to. For example, you might want to look at staff leave, to start planning so that everybody doesn't suddenly want to go away at the same time.

Or if you are involved in a long-term project where some elements need to be finished before you start others, your helicopter view will help you to mesh all this in with the other things that will be happening in your life at the same time.

EFFECTIVE FORWARD PLANNING
PLACES TO BE

In fact, almost all '**Places to Be**' entries are associated with a '**Thing to Do**'. You only go to the school because you need to pick up your kids, or to a cafe because you have arranged to meet someone. This is where co-ordination between your various diaries is essential, if you are keeping your diaries on paper – and where electronic diaries often score by letting you keep different kinds of information in one place.

When you are considering your **Places to Be**, you will be looking at the time you need to allow for travel, and any other preparations you might need to make for the event you are travelling to. You will also be able to factor

in elements which might affect your ability to be in the right place at the right time – roadworks on the A32, predictable rush-hour congestion, a threatened train strike.

There is no point knowing where you are supposed to be if you get lost on the way. This is where technology really can help. If you have access to a computer, or even better to a smartphone, mapping software can tell you exactly where to go, how to get there and how long it will take. Great! But don't be fooled – remember the secret element built into all information technology to ensure that when it really matters the battery dies and there is no mobile phone coverage. OK, maybe I'm being a little cynical, but you get the idea – always leave a little more time than you think you need!

The same applies if you use a good old street atlas or local knowledge to get around. Trains are late, traffic gets jammed and shoe-heels break. You can't plan for unexpected delays – and usually, things work pretty well. But try to build in a little extra time to get to where you need to be, and aim to arrive a few minutes early. You will avoid a lot of stress, and give yourself a breathing space to make sure you're poised and ready for the task in hand.

I can see for miles and miles.
THE WHO

EFFECTIVE FORWARD PLANNING
THINGS TO DO

Everything that you need to do – either because you have made a commitment, or because someone else has tasked you – should be in your **Things to Do** diary. Make sure that they are all properly transferred to the appropriate Terrain Maps – and remember that you may need to enter some tasks on more than one day, or that there may be follow-ups which have to be noted.

Some **Things to Do** entries will be just that: something that you can do from almost anywhere, like calling someone on your mobile or buying a newspaper. They may not even have a specific time allocated to them – so long as you do them sometime during the day, that's all you need. Others may have deadlines (post letters before the postbox is emptied) or very precise times (collect car at 4.30).

The important thing to get clear at the start is whether your entries and the time you allow for them – in both **Places to Be** and **Things to Do** - rcfcr just to the actual task or place itself, or to any other time-consuming activities associated with them. To give a simple example: if you need to pick up your children from school, will you put in simply 'Children from school, 3.30', or will you add in the time it will take you to get ready to leave the house, travel to school and come back home? It doesn't matter: you may prefer either format, but if you simply put in the actual time when you need to be at the school gate, then you must either make separate entries for the associated activities, or co-ordinate very closely between your two diaries. Otherwise you are liable to find that you are committed to doing something with no time to prepare for it or travel to it!

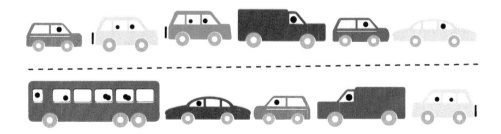

EFFECTIVE FORWARD PLANNING
PEOPLE

Most of the entries on your Terrain Maps will involve dealing with people – people you intend to meet or talk to on the phone, people who will be supplying you with services, people you need to do things for. All of these transactions may be made easier and more pleasant if you are able to relate in some way to the people involved.

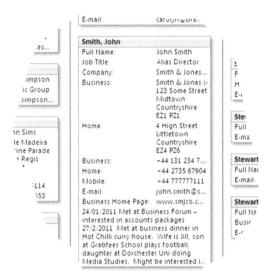

It is well known that the subject most people like to talk about most is themselves. If, when you meet someone – over a table or even just over a shop counter – you are able to bring in something to demonstrate that you consider them as people, not simply as parts of a business transaction, then the chances are that you will do better in your negotiation or receive better service. To put it bluntly, people prefer to deal with others they like – and treat them better. And you are not simply improving your own outcome and making yourself more popular – you are also making the other person's day better. It's a win-win situation!

This is why it is important to keep your **People Folders** up to date. It doesn't take long to note that 'Eric's daughter having baby – due end March' – but it might mean quite a lot to Eric if you ask about her health next time.

Unlike diary entries, your information about people doesn't date quickly and will keep on growing as you add to it. That is why you don't normally try to incorporate it into your Terrain Maps: there's too much of it, and it would be a waste of time to be constantly transferring it about the place. Instead, your Terrain Map will note who you are meeting, when and where. At a convenient time beforehand you can consult your **People Folders** to refresh your memory with any relevant information.

As you can see, **TRIM** works by making sure that you always co-ordinate the information you have stored about what you should be doing at any given moment, where you need to be to do it, and what you should know about anyone you'll be dealing with. Conceptually, you keep all these various elements in separate compartments and different places, and it may be that you find it easiest to do just that by having physical diaries and folders. But this is the kind of co-ordination that computers are good at, and you may well find that in practice you can run everything on a computer or even a smartphone. We'll look more closely at this in Chapter 10.

STUFF HAPPENS...

The **Weekly Helicopter Trip** is much more than just a diary-planning exercise. It's a real chance to look at what's happening in your life.

Did last week turn out like you thought it would? What happened that you didn't predict or plan for? Good or bad? Are these things going to keep on affecting life for the next week – or two weeks, or more?

If last week's events were unwelcome as well as unplanned, what would you like to do about them for the future? Are you going to live with them, or do something to prevent them affecting your life again? If they are unavoidable, what can you change to make you feel better about them? And if you decide you can't do anything at all – then relax. At least you don't have to worry about trying!

Of course if your unexpected events were serendipity – work out how you can keep them coming and incorporate them into your plans for future weeks!

EFFECTIVE FORWARD PLANNING
VISUALISING AND REHEARSING

Now that you have your coming week planned out in front of you, what else can you do to prepare for it?

So far all you have done is make a list of **Places to Be** and **Things to Do** – a great start and essential to guarantee that you are always in the right place, with all your tasks completed. But really effective planning can take you a stage further – and ensure that so far as possible your meetings and activities have outcomes which help you to achieve your short, medium and long-term goals.

This is where visualising and mentally rehearsing comes in. What you need to do is think – one at a time – of all the meetings, conversations and activities which you have scheduled for the coming week.

As you consider each meeting, visualise where it will take place and what is likely to happen. If it's with someone you have already met, then you probably already know and can bring to mind the location where the meeting will happen. Is it in an office, a restaurant, a coffee bar? Formal or informal? Relaxed and friendly, or slightly confrontational – over a desk, maybe? Will you have a choice of where to sit? If it is a formal meeting with several people, will you know them all? Can you find out more about them before the meeting? Will you be asked to introduce yourself?

Is there anyone in particular you should try to speak to before the meeting? (Remember to add this in to your Terrain Maps!)

Having visualised where the meeting will take place, who will be involved and what part you are likely to play, the next step is to mentally rehearse what will happen. Will you need some smalltalk before the business starts? If so, do you know enough about the person you will be meeting to talk sensibly about their family or activities? Have they done anything recently that you should know about, to mention or avoid? If you will be asked to introduce yourself, you need to sound confident and make a good first impression. What will you say? If there are minutes of a previous meeting – or even if you're just meeting a friend who you last saw a couple of months ago – is there anything that you undertook to do last time which you'll need to talk about? Is there anything that you are particularly proud of, that you want to make sure everyone hears about? How will you introduce the subject?

Most meetings, however informal or inconsequential, have an outcome of some kind. What would you like the outcome of this meeting to be? How do you need to steer the conversation to make sure that you come away with the right result?

So many questions! But in practice, most meetings will be simple and need little visualisation or mental rehearsal. The ones that do, though, will really benefit from a bit of forethought. You will feel more relaxed and confident going into the meeting, and because of that you will perform better. You may even have a little smile as the person you are meeting plays her part just as you mentally rehearsed it – but don't get too confident, because they will probably produce some completely unforeseen item out of left field at some point!

THE WEEKLY HELICOPTER TRIP

FLIGHT PLAN: EQUIPMENT & SCHEDULE
POINT OF DEPARTURE: 24 OCTOBER
DESTINATION: 06 NOVEMBER

1

TERRAIN MAPS
You can use your old Terrain Maps to review what you did over the past week, or just check the main points in your diaries. You'll need new blank sheets to plan ahead.

2

DIARIES
You will be using your diaries (or smart phone, or Outlook Calendar, or whatever) to provide the raw material for the next fortnight's Terrain Maps – meetings, to-do's, appointments, family commitments....

3

EFFECTIVE FORWARD PLANNING
Remember – that's the only purpose of this **Helicopter Trip**. Be realistic about what you can actually plan for – leave a bit of space for the Incoming Fire that's bound to hit you as days go by.

And DON'T start doing stuff now! You're up here to plan, not take action!

4

TERRAIN MAPPING
By the end of the Trip, you should have Terrain Maps for the full period that you're looking ahead. Some of the territory may be pretty uncharted, with not many definite features – but your Terrain Maps will show you the framework of commitments that you're going to have to build your other activities round.

5

MENTAL VISUALISATION
Your Terrain Maps will point up the main challenges that you'll likely face over the next period. Now's the time to look forward and start thinking how they will actually feel for you – and how you might want to change the experience. This will lead to ....

6

MENTAL REHEARSALS
....when, over the time before the meeting, interview or whatever takes place, you will work out what you would like to happen and what you need to do to achieve your objectives.

BRIEFING THE PILOT

The **Weekly Helicopter Trip** is for your benefit, and yours alone – so you must feel absolutely free to modify it to suit your own requirements. This is the area, more than most, where your choice of how you record your diary and background information will be important. So long as you are able to store, retrieve and match up all the necessary detail about **Places to Be**, **Things to Do** and **People** and **Subjects** you will be dealing with, it's entirely up to you how you do it. Personally I prefer to use mainly paper, but probably most of the people I have trained now use a mixture of paper and electronic media. As you will see in Chapter 10, electronic diaries and notebooks have their limitations – but they can be very effective in letting you switch between diaries and background information quickly and accurately from anywhere at any time.

As the **TRIM** techniques become more familiar and you use them more intuitively, you will develop your own methods of working and ways of using the different elements. Everyone has their own requirements, though the basics remain the same.

The main tool that is essential to make the TRIM system effective is the Terrain Map**, and however you structure your records and planning you need to end up with** Maps **for up to the next two weeks. They will be the indispensable guide to your daily activities.**

Broken into all of its parts and written down, the **Weekly Helicopter Trip** looks complex and time-consuming. Believe me – it's not. I reckon that my normal **Weekly Trip** takes around 25 minutes – to check diaries, update existing and complete new **Terrain Maps**, Visualise and Mentally Rehearse meetings. Of course some of these things – particularly Visualisation and Mental Rehearsal – can be done only briefly at this stage, and in more detail as the meeting in question approaches. For that reason you will probably want to schedule some time in your **Terrain Maps** specifically to mentally rehearse particular meetings: but it's really useful to start off now, because quite often these processes spark questions or actions that need research or extra preparation and you might as well know about that now. You will also benefit from your brain's subconscious efforts – I'm sure that you have had the experience that even when you are not consciously thinking about a project, your mind has been turning it over and related thoughts have popped up quite unexpectedly. A little mental rehearsal will stimulate this process. Of course, as always, the important thing is to be prepared to capture these valuable thoughts when they arise! Otherwise you will find yourself in the frustrating position of knowing that you had a great idea, but not quite remembering what it was...

The **Weekly Helicopter Trip**, and its input to **Terrain Maps** for the coming two weeks, are at the heart of the **TRIM** system. You can modify the technique, the materials and the product almost infinitely to suit your own ways of working, storing information and dealing with people and subjects: but the basic principle of systematically taking a good look at what is coming up, feeding it into daily schedules with easy access to all the information you need for each day's activities, and trying to anticipate as much as possible about how they will actually happen, is the very key to taking control of your life. In the course of the exercise you are able to check that what you are doing is helping you to achieve your personal goals – short, medium and long-term. If not, this is your opportunity to do something about it! And if all is going roughly as it should be – what a great way to motivate yourself to do more of the same!

As senior partner in a growing advertising company, one of Anne Elliott's main responsibilities is to pitch for sales from new customers, often at Board level. For Anne, the exercise of systematically looking a couple of weeks ahead has become essential.

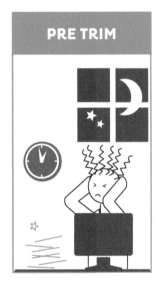

PRE TRIM

Anne confesses that she is not the most organised person when it comes to planning things – not unusual for someone in the creative industries! "If I have a big meeting coming up, of course I have the meeting date noted in the diary and I know I'll be there. But although I am well aware that there's always masses of other preparation to be done – including making sure other people have their material ready in time – for some reason I always used to find myself working into the small hours the night before the meeting. At the presentation I often felt I was flying by the seat of my pants, and afterwards I invariably felt I could have made a better impression if I had just got my act together better beforehand."

WITH TRIM

When Anne got into the routine of **Weekly Helicopter Trips** she suddenly found it was much easier to prepare for big meetings and presentations. "Although the **Weekly Helicopter Trip** is mainly about planning ahead," she says, "in fact what it really helped me to do was to 'plan back' from a big meeting. Because I was looking at the whole process a couple of weeks ahead, rather than just noting that I had to be somewhere on a certain day, I was able to really make sure that all the different inputs were ready on time and fitted together properly. My sales pitches are measurably more successful and I feel a whole lot better about the whole process."

Now when Anne has a major presentation to make, she notes all the various elements – advertisement copy and storyboards from copywriters, artwork from the designers, financial aspects from the accountant as well as her own input of fitting it all together and writing a presentation – on a sheet, along with the dates when they all need to be ready for her. The helicopter view shows what else is supposed to be happening in the next few weeks (Anne normally looks a month ahead to note big presentations coming up) and whether any major clashes need to be averted. The process of transferring the information to daily Terrain Maps for the next fortnight crystallises what needs to be done and lets Anne monitor the work of others involved. Finally, it makes sure that she puts everything together two days before the big meeting – not early in the morning of the same day!

As Anne says: "I suppose it's a bit like project planning in a way – you identify an end-point where all sorts of inputs need to have been completed and put in order. But it would be crazy to run a full project-management routine every time I need to put a sales pitch together. The **Weekly Helicopter Trip** does the trick of identifying all the elements I need and putting a date on them. I always know where I am and what has to be done."

"I always know where I am & what has to be done"

Hello World!

Interactions

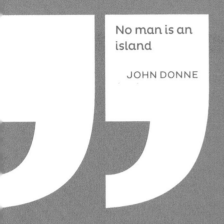

No man is an island

JOHN DONNE

INTERACTIONS ARE WHAT IT'S ALL ABOUT

Every day your life is changed – guided, made better, made worse, made easier, made more fun – by Interactions.

Look at it another way. If you roll a big ball bearing across a huge, flat area with no friction – maybe across an ice rink – then it will just keep rolling in a straight line for ever. That's how life might be without Interactions – kind of tranquil but boring.

Now think of the same steel ball in a pinball machine. It gets fired up a chute, then bounces off bumpers, flippers and lights until finally it disappears down the final exit. In fact, everything that happens to it is an Interaction, and each Interaction has an effect on the play.

If you live in some sort of corporate hell, you might almost think of your day as a sort of pinball machine. Your alarm kicks you into activity, then for the next 12 hours you are reacting to all sorts of outside events till you eventually escape to bed and slumber....

Of course this is a huge exaggeration! You are not a pinball and your life is not controlled by someone pressing flipper buttons. But I hope you see what I'm getting at – almost everything we do is in response to an Interaction with another person or an object ("the printer's not working - again...") From the moment we get up in the morning until we go to sleep at night, we go through a constant series of Interactions.

SO WHAT IS AN 'INTERACTION'?

We are constantly surrounded by people and things demanding that we do "something". People make direct contact – suppliers, customers, family, friends, colleagues, bosses, staff, all need to tell you something, or ask you to do something. Babies cry. You get emails, phonecalls, letters, tweets, texts, all bombarding you with information and requests. You watch TV, read a newspaper or magazine, look at Facebook, and absorb more information which is useful and might help you work towards your goals – but which might also need a response. Finally, the washing machine stops – you need to unload it. The fuel warning light comes on in the car.

Some of these pressures are urgent, some obviously not. Some demand action from us straight away. Others are passive, simply providing information which we need to store away for use sometime in the future.

And then there is a third, special kind of Interactions. In the midst of all this maelstrom of information and demands for action coming in from outside, your own brain keeps generating even more '**Things to Do**'.

We are all brilliant thinkers. We have inspirations which make Archimedes' Eureka moment in the bath look simple. From the sudden realisation that you really *should* dye your hair blonde, to simply remembering that you need to buy teabags on the way home, your brain is constantly giving you instructions.

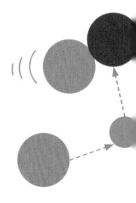

Of course we can ignore these imperious demands for attention. We are human beings. We have free will! But life is real – and we know that if some demands are ignored, bad things will happen to us. We constantly have to make decisions about which ones to respond to, and when. How well we deal with our Interactions will define how effectively we travel towards our goals. **TRIM** provides the tools to deal with all these Interactions and set the right course – for ourselves!

SO HOW DO WE INTERACT WITH INTERACTIONS?

Have a look at the picture opposite.

The top half, in orange, is about the *actions* which might be generated by an Interaction. When you walk away after having a meeting with someone, you might know that you now have a '**Place to Be**', or a '**Thing to Do**' – or both. "Could you email that report to me, and come and discuss it next Tuesday?" "Let's both pick a team, then we can meet in the Rat and Ferret at 6.30 to finalise it."

These things are normally about *efficiency* – they are about 'quantity', or 'getting things done'. They don't only come from people directly – they might arrive in the form of emails, magazine articles or even an advert you see on the Tube. Or, of course, from the idea factory in your brain! Whatever the source, they all demand activity at some time or another.

In the lower part of the picture is the non-action result of an Interaction – the production of *information*. This is where *effectiveness* or 'quality' comes in. The word information of course covers a huge range of possibilities: Sharon's had her baby, the shop's closing in half an hour, tax on petrol has gone up 5p, we need to have the Acorn Project finished by six o'clock, the Acorn Project manager is going on holiday for six weeks....

It is quite probable, even likely, that the same Interactions will also have generated *actions* – a congratulations card for Sharon, hurry to finish the shopping, fill up with petrol, work out how to finish the project or get on without the manager.

What is important about all of these possible outcomes from each Interaction is that you *capture* them effectively. You will need to do something about the actions – probably not straight away, but quite possibly at some specified future time. And you need to store the information, so that it is in the right place and accessible next time you need it – when you meet Sharon in the supermarket, or go to a meeting to discuss Project Acorn.

Do you remember that right at the beginning of the book I promised that if you use **TRIM** properly, you'll never forget a meeting or break a commitment? Well, making sure that you capture the outcomes of your Interactions is the key to keeping my promise.

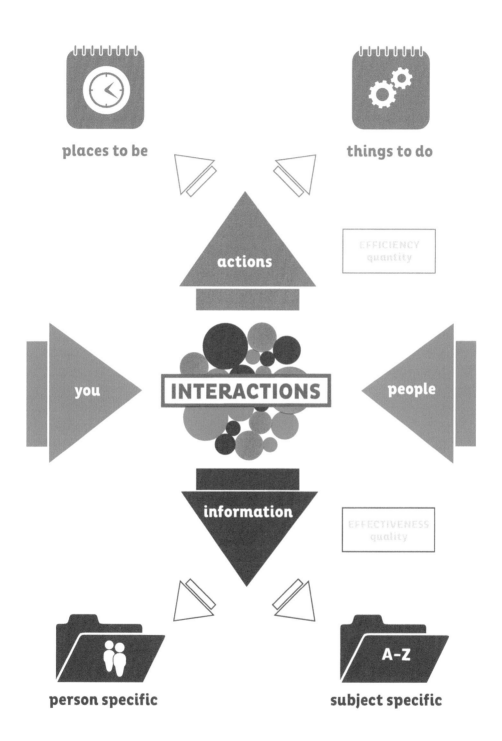

places to be

things to do

actions

EFFICIENCY
quantity

you

INTERACTIONS

people

information

EFFECTIVENESS
quality

person specific

subject specific

A–Z

CAPTURING THE RESULTS

'Capturing the outcomes' might sound rather daunting, as if the outcomes have escaped and are wandering around waiting to bite you. All it means is making sure that all the essential details, of actions and information, get properly stored where they won't get lost or forgotten about. If they simply evaporate after your Interaction, you may only see the consequences later, when you discover that you have failed to meet a commitment or made some undertaking that you can't possibly fulfil. Then they *will* have bitten you!

So how are you going to do that? In fact, it's a two-stage process. The first essential – and it really is an essential – is to make sure you have some way of recording it at the time, or at least *straight after the event*. How often have you thought "Oh, I must remember that..." and then either forgotten about it altogether, or been unable to think of the main points you needed to act on?

Unfortunately, even if it has been properly trained, human memory is a very fallible recording mechanism. Certainly, some people have quite extraordinary memories and are able to reel off strings of numbers or names without difficulty. But that's what they are – extraordinary.

For most of us, it's just not worth relying on keeping stuff in our heads for three main reasons:

1 we're liable to forget

2 even if we don't forget, we're cluttering up useful mind storage!

3 our wonderfully evolved brains are designed to 'add value' to information, not just store it

However, this is where technology really is beginning to catch up. If you have a smart phone or tablet computer or an iPad or iPhone with Siri, you can instantly dictate a note which will then be available on your phone or desktop, or can be sent to you automatically by email. Of course the system isn't perfect, and some of my attempts to tell Siri what to write have ended in hilarious (or on one occasion embarrassing) results. But the software really does get better as you use it more: and it normally produces something good enough to jog your memory, which is often all that's required.

Alternatively you can type in notes, and while this can sometimes be a laborious process it shares the advantage with voice recognition apps that later on, if you need to, you can cut and paste entries to use in a diary or folder.

Any smartphone or tablet will let you create a 'voice memo', which is simply a recording of your own voice. This is fine so long as you don't want to use the information anywhere else – and it can be a bit of a pain to find the right 'memo' as they are often only identified by the date and time when the memo was recorded.

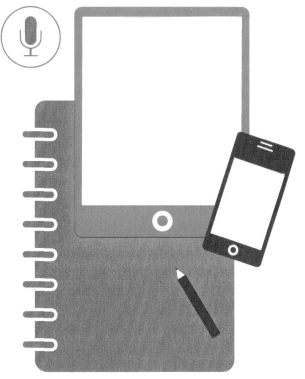

And finally, of course, there's good old pen and paper. I have always been in the habit of carrying an A4 pad with me wherever I go, and in many ways I still find it the most convenient and reliable way of capturing the outcomes of Interactions. It's cheap, it doesn't need batteries, and it's easy to use. What's not to like? Of course not everyone likes to lug around an A4 pad everywhere – and it can look a bit obvious if you immediately start writing notes as your casual contact walks off! But I can draw diagrams, use different colours and underline, cross out or insert chunks of text. All I have to do is be able to read my writing! Of course, the technology to allow my 'pen' to transfer my writing into electronic text and pictures is already available – though it still has a way to go to become reliable enough for everyday use.

Many people, particularly engineers and IT professionals, like to use a 'daybook' – often a thick, A4-size hardback notebook which they simply use to record any thoughts, phone numbers, conversations, calculations or whatever. Adding the date every now and again makes it easy to search, and when it's full it's easy to store a few 'back numbers' on a bookshelf.

A PLACE FOR EVERYTHING
(AND EVERYTHING IN ITS PLACE)

Interactions, whether with people, things or just your own brain, often generate demands for action on your part – to go somewhere, do something, or quite often both. When your best customer says "Let's have lunch on Thursday," that obviously means that you have a **Place to Be**: but it may also mean that you need to work out what she wants from you, and plan how you are going to respond when she asks for a 20% price reduction on next month's order.

When you walk away, or put the phone down after an Interaction like this, the first priority is to note these actions in your appropriate diaries – '**Places to Be**' and '**Things to Do**'. Of course, as always these may well be one and the same place. The important point is that you have an unmissable reminder that you have something to do, and when you've got to do it.

Of course, in virtually every case you will already have looked at your '**Places to Be**' diary before agreeing to a new **Place to Be**! So adding the new item is simple and quick.

If the new engagement is within the time frame of your current Terrain Maps, you can also put it in there: otherwise it will appear in a future **Weekly Helicopter Trip**.

If the new action is a '**Thing to Do**', you can also add that to your Terrain Map if the timing is right – for example "I'll give you a call this afternoon, before 4.30". If it's outwith your Terrain Map timing, put it in your '**Things to Do**' diary: "I'll give you a call in a couple of months".

You don't need to 'double up' on your '**Things to Do**' diary and your Terrain Map unless it's really important and you want to make extra sure – "I'll give you a call next Monday" might go in both.

'X' MARKS THE SPOT

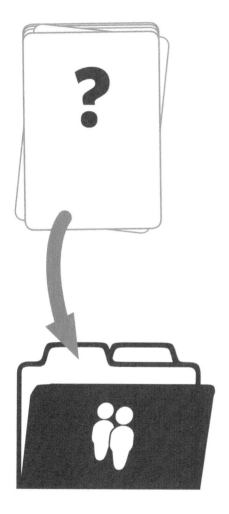

Think of the traditional pirate's treasure map – in fact, it's just a simple device for storing information to recover buried booty. The main purpose of storing *any* information is to be able to retrieve and use it later – so whatever technique or technology you use, this has to be the first consideration. There is nothing more frustrating than knowing that you have the information you need *somewhere*, but not quite knowing where that somewhere is!

With **People Specific** information, there's not usually a problem. Of course, you need to decide which people you actually want to keep information about – as a rule, those who specially matter to you, for business or personal reasons. The idea is to keep information that is going to enhance your relationship with that person. Generally speaking, this is pretty much the kind of information you would like to think they might want to remember about you! Many business people – especially if they are involved in sales – do this as a matter of course, and a whole industry selling 'Customer Relationship Management' systems has developed. But the principle is exactly the same for any relationship that's important to you, whether it's helping you to advance your career or be a better Mum.

Whether you use an old-fashioned Rolodex filer or the latest Microsoft technology, you can normally just add new information to a person's individual **People Folder**. Some systems provide convenient divisions for contact details, personal details like birthdays, and so on: but what you normally need is simply a dedicated space where you can note relevant information that you may want to recall when you next meet the person concerned. We'll look in Chapter 10 at the various electronic possibilities.

As time goes on and you add more information, you will find it easy to decide which products of your Interaction are relevant and deserve to be recorded, and which are ephemeral and can be discarded: you don't want to waste time writing down stuff which is of no interest either to you or to your contact! On the other hand, as the person's record grows, you will probably find that they are amazed and impressed by your superb memory (and interest in them!) when you ask them how they got on with something they were doing six months ago!

Of course, you need to make a judgement not only about what information is relevant, but also whether it is the kind of information that you are comfortable storing. The Golden Rule is never to store information that you would not want the person concerned to know that you are storing. Some information – about things like a person's religion, sexuality, race or health – is officially classified as 'sensitive' and keeping formal records of it could contravene Data Protection legislation. As a general rule you should never reveal personal information about one person to anyone else, or allow them to have access to your person records. If in doubt – don't!

Subject specific information may present more problems in deciding where to file it, because often an Interaction will generate data which is relevant to many different subjects. The simple answer is to copy it to all the relevant subject folders: but this creates its own difficulties, the main one being that you have a life to live and you don't want to spend all night writing notes or standing over the photocopier! You need to be sensible, and plan your **Subject Folders** with a bit of care. If some information is obviously relevant to a wide range of subjects, put it in its own folder where you can refer to it easily. You might want to create groups of subjects – projects for one client, children's education, family birthdays – each of which might need a couple of 'common' folders holding information relevant to every subject in the group.

By now, if you have battled through this far, you are probably clutching your head and convinced that I am trying to turn you into a glorified minute writer and filing clerk. "Nothing could be further from the truth, my dear...."

Dealing with Interactions, and proper and effective information storage, are vital elements of **TRIM**. They are the disciplines that make sure that you never break your promises or fail to fulfil your commitments, and perform to the best of your abilities. But they don't have to be a pain in the neck.

Let's look at a couple of ways of making them more fun.

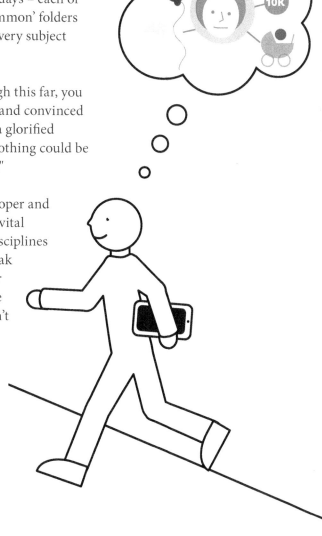

MAP THAT IDEA...

Developed by Tony Buzan in the BBC's *Use Your Head* series
in the 1970s, Mind Mapping has become a recognised way
of visually outlining information. Starting with one central
theme or concept, further elements of information are
linked to it, and to each other, to demonstrate connections
and patterns which would not be obvious in a written
description. The easiest way of explaining Mind Mapping is
with an example.

As you can see, the main categories and connections are
closest to the central idea, and other groups and sub-groups
radiate off them. You can use colours, symbols, words
and shapes to make groups and connections. Visual
representations are easier to understand, generate new ideas
and can reveal unexpected relationships.

Mind Mapping can be used for planning, note-taking, organising information effectively, problem-solving and design. In **TRIM**, it is especially useful in helping to bring together separate elements of information and action which all affect one particular project or problem.

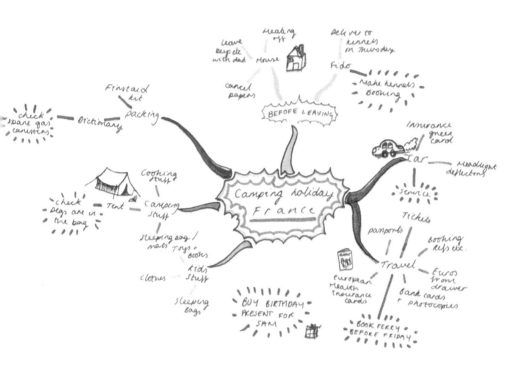

Mind Maps can simply be hand-drawn using coloured pens and imagination; or you can download many simple, free programs and apps to use on a PC or Notepad. Personally I find it easier to use a computer app, because it is easier to organise my ideas that way: two excellent programs are FreeMind (freemind. sourceforge.net) and iThoughts for the iPad – but there are lots.

There are plenty of books which claim to tell you how to use Mind Mapping – but for me, one of the main advantages is that it's a very personal technique. There's no right or wrong way to do it – just do what comes naturally. It's well worth a try.

LET'S PLAY DESKS

If you normally work at a desk, many of your Interactions will take place there – phone calls, emails, maybe even meetings (and certainly, recording the actions that follow them!) The way you organise your desk can make a huge difference to your efficiency and effectiveness. But even if the nearest you ever get to a desk is opening your mail at the kitchen table, many of the principles are the same.

Let's start off with an actual desk. What's the best way of laying it out?

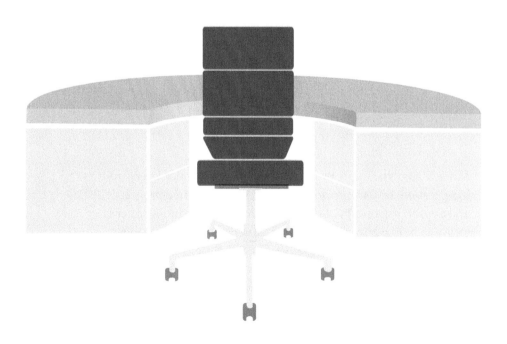

Some items are essential.
First of all, you will almost certainly have a...

1 COMPUTER SCREEN & KEYBOARD
If you do, I'd bet that at present they take centre stage
– the keyboard right in front of you, and the screen
behind it, but still in the middle of the desk.

Unless you spend almost all your time using the computer,
why is it taking up the best parts of the valuable real estate in
your working environment? Do you do most of your reading
on-screen, or from real old-fashioned paper? When you want to
make notes, or organise papers, or check your bank statement,
do you do it online – or do you find yourself having to move
your keyboard out of the way, and balance it on a pile of papers
to make space to work in?

If you can, shift the balance of power. Your computer works
for you and it doesn't need to be set up to be worshipped on
an altar! Of course, if you do use the computer constantly for
writing, research and so on – if it's your main tool – then you
might well need it in the middle of the desk. But if not, try
moving it to one side, and putting the monitor on a raised tray
so that you can slide the keyboard underneath when you're not
using it. If you have the main 'box' of the computer on the desk,
see if you can move it to a side table or put it on the floor. You
may be amazed how your view changes – and how much extra
working space you suddenly seem to have!

An alternative, of course, is a laptop or tablet
computer. Neither of these is particularly good
if you do a lot of serious IT-based work (though
lots of journalists work entirely from laptops):
and if you start adding full-size keyboards and
monitors, you end up being worse off than with
a full-size PC. However, if you just need to read
emails and do a bit of web-browsing and social
networking, a small computer may be ideal.

What's next?

2 ### THE PHONE!

One or more phones used to be an essential status symbol on every executive's desk – the more the better! Fortunately, that's all different now. Most people need just one phone for 'business' or 'at home' calls, and a mobile for when they are out and about – indeed, many people no longer bother with a landline phone. If you don't expect to receive constant phonecalls, why clutter up your desk with a phone at all? With a wireless phone you can give yourself some much-needed exercise by putting it on a table away from your desk, and strolling round the room when you answer a call. And you can keep your mobile in your pocket!

3 ### THE MOST IMPORTANT ITEMS ON YOUR DESK...

will be the brightly painted lump of clay your daughter presented you with after her art class, the stone you picked up on the beach to remind you of that romantic holiday in Greece, and the model of the Ferrari that you will be driving when you get rich.

Next after these, however, will be the things you use to record interactions and give you instant access to information.

4 First, of course, will be your TERRAIN MAP FOR TODAY – and maybe one or two more for coming days so that you can note any new items as they crop up.

5 Then, if you use paper for these, you will have your DIARIES: **Places to Be** & **Things to Do** and maybe FOLDERS for the **Key People** you know that you will be dealing with today. You'll want to have all of these at your fingertips so that you can consult or update them without having to scrabble around looking for them. Try to keep them upright, in a box or between bookends, so that they take up as little space as possible on the desk.

6 Then, finally, there are your STACKS

Stacks are simply piles of stuff that you create – or that create themselves – as temporary information stores for the things that you are currently focusing on. You can organise them any way you like: by project, or place, or time, or people. The only important word there is *organise*! It's childishly easy to have piles of paper all over your desk – but unless it is organised, it's simply clutter and you will spend more time looking for the bit of paper you want than actually using it. You can find an invoice for Project Pluto widgets very easily in the Project Pluto stack, but it's a recipe for frustration if you have to search through random heaps of stuff about everything from little Mandy's birthday party to renewing the insurance on your house...

The computer can be a huge help in desk-taming – especially useful if you don't have a desk. All of your diaries and folders can be on there, taking up no space at all and instantly accessible (until the computer crashes – you need to have a plan...) But even then, unless you've gone completely digital, you will want to have your Terrain Map and probably a few Stacks around your desk.

Any way you look at it, the central focus of your desk space should be YOU. You know exactly where you'll be sitting (and I'm sure you are always careful to follow the best ergonomic advice to ensure that your posture and position are correct!) Whatever else you keep on the desk, make sure that you always have a clear working area exactly in front of you. Don't let anything else encroach on it – no papers, staplers, boxes of business cards, or any of the general junk that seems to accumulate from nowhere. Your desk drawers are the best place for most of these – with an occasional clear-out to ditch all the bits you haven't used or consulted for the last six months.

So there you are, Captain Kirk in command of the Starship Enterprise, hurtling through the day, dodging asteroids and dealing with all the incoming fire along the way.

➡ You need to know where the controls are
➡ You need to be able to get to the right ones, quickly and accurately
➡ You need to know where you are going – so your **Terrain Map** is in front of you
➡ You need to anticipate and make the best of all your Interactions
➡ You need to capture the outcomes and deal with them effectively

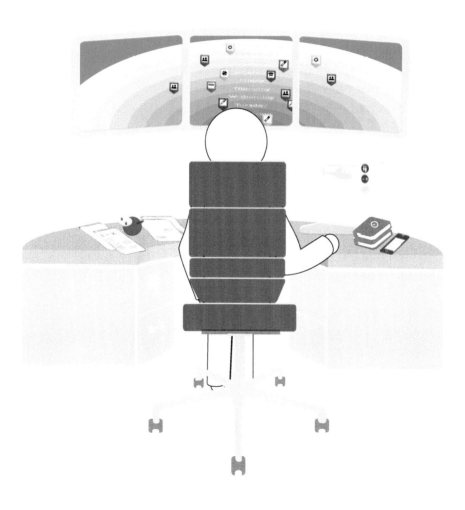

And you thought organising your desk would be boring!

THE OTHER SIDE OF INTERACTIONS

When your Interactions involve other people, and not just inputs from the TV, or emails, or your own brain, then the outcomes will very often involve actions by the other person. When you meet Tony and part by saying "OK, let's meet for lunch next Thursday at Gianni's Bistro," that produces a commitment not only for you but for Tony too.

What happens if you know that Tony has the attention span of a gnat and the memory of a goldfish? What are the chances that you will turn up at the Bistro and find yourself on your own? What do you do about it?

You don't want to double your own workload by providing them with detailed notes of what you agreed – but on the other hand you don't want to waste your time either. Nor do you want to appear nagging or distrustful! The only sensible course of action is to be aware of the problem, and do whatever is the minimum necessary to make sure that the other person at least remembers their commitments – even if you can't force them to fulfil them. You'll be making a note for yourself anyway, so a quick email immediately after the Interaction confirming the arrangement (and maybe re-stating any other key points agreed) will be very little extra effort. You are not producing 'minutes of the meeting' – so don't waste your time replicating the whole Interaction in a different format! And if you still think that Tony is capable of forgetting to come for lunch, a short email in the morning – maybe on the pretext that you 'may be five minutes late' – will jog his memory!

Alternatively, of course, you could give Tony a copy of this excellent volume, or send him on a **TRIM** course...

SO WHAT HAVE YOU LEARNED ABOUT INTERACTIONS?

Your life is a constant avalanche of Interactions
– with other people in meetings, phone calls and
correspondence, with press, TV and other media,
and with your own thoughts and ideas.

You need a way to handle all this activity.

→ Always have your **Terrain Map** handy

→ Make sure you can always capture the outcomes of
   Interactions immediately, wherever you go. Pen and paper
   are hard to beat.

→ Transfer actions and information to the right places as soon as you can

→ Refer to the relevant folders for whatever, or whoever, you are dealing with

→ Update these folders after each Interaction

If you follow these simple principles, you will soon
find that you are less rushed, more in control, and
better able to cope with what life throws at you!

TRIM

Under the Bonnet

More about Relationships,
Information and Management –
and a bit about Time...

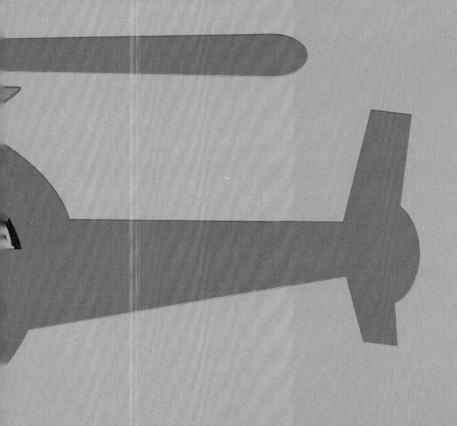

I may not be
the world's
best manager,
but I'm in the
top one

BRIAN CLOUGH

TRIM

RELATIONSHIPS

Relationships matter – more than anything else.

As we saw in the last chapter, Interactions shape your activities through the day – what you do, and how you do it.

Relationships are what make things work – the oil that helps the cogs of our lives mesh smoothly together, without grinding or sticking.

Relationships can also make our activities more fun. Galley slaves and Varsity boat crews probably both work just as hard. What makes the activity more enjoyable for the students is that their bond with the cox is better than the slaves' strained relationship with the men with whips!

The only rule

The fundamental principle for any successful relationship was expressed in the Bible over two thousand years ago:

DO UNTO OTHERS AS YOU WOULD HAVE THEM DO UNTO YOU.

In fact, as the opposite page shows, all of the major world religions teach very much the same message.

THE GOLDEN RULE

HINDUISM

This is the sum of duty: do not do to others what would cause pain if done to you

Mahabharata 5:1517

BAHA'I FAITH

Lay not on any soul a load that you would not wish to be laid upon you, and desire not for anyone the things you would no desire for yourself

Baha'u'llah Gleanings

ISLAM

Not one of you truly believes until you wish for others what you wish for yourself

The Prophet Muhammad, Hadith

JUDAISM

What is hateful to you, do not do to your neighbour. This is the whole Torah; all the rest is commentary

Hillel, Talmud, Shabbat 31a

JAINISM

One should treat all creatures in the world as one would like to be treated

Mahavira Sutrakritanga

ZOROASTRIANISM

Do not do unto others whatever is injurious to yourself

Shayast-na-Shayast 13.29

NATIVE SPIRITUALITY

We are as much alive as we keep the earth alive

Chief Dan George

UNITARIANISM

We affirm and promote respect for the interdependent web of all existence of which we are a part

Unitarian principle

TAOISM

Regard your neighbours gain as your own gain, and your neighbours loss as your own loss

T'ai Shang Kan Ying P'ien

SIKHISM

I am a stranger to no one; and no one is a stranger to me. indeed, I am a friend to all

Guru Granth Sahib, pg. 1299

CHRISTIANITY

In everything, do to others as you would have them do to you; for this is the law and the prophets.

Jesus, Matthew 7:12

CONFUCIANISM

One word which sums up all the basis of all good conduct... loving kindness. Do not do to others what you do not want done to yourself.

Confucius Analects 15.23

BUDDHISM

Treat not others in ways that you yourself would find hurtful

Udana-Varga 5.18

Of course you don't need to be religious. If you're atheist or agnostic, or simply don't care, just ask yourself the question:

WOULD I DO THIS TO MY MUM? MY DAD? MY LOVER? MY CHILDREN?

If the answer is "No!" – then why do it to anyone else?

The principle is universal, and it doesn't matter who the 'others' are. They might be family, friends, business contacts or even people you have never met – your interactions with them will always be more successful if you speak and act towards them in the way you would like them to deal with you.

We have all experienced infuriating and frustrating calls to call centres. We end the call feeling angry and badly served – and poor customer service is the main reason companies lose customers. The reason for our frustration is not that we have received a poor-quality product, but because the person we were speaking to didn't treat us properly – maybe they came over as unhelpful, or 'wooden', or even just plain rude.

But think of the (occasional!) times when the call-centre person really gives the impression that they care about your problems and are doing their best to be helpful. Don't you feel better about them – and the company? You may be no closer to resolving your difficulties, but at least you have the impression that somebody is concerned about them, and you're much more likely to give them the benefit of the doubt.

Of course it's a two-way street. The person at the other end of the phone will also respond more positively if you treat them the way you would like them to treat you – politely and with respect.

It's impossible to overemphasise how important this principle is. In virtually every contact you make with another human being (and indeed with many animals – ask any animal trainer!) your experience will be more positive and productive if you are nice to them. You can sum up the whole thing in two words:

Be pleasant!

This may sound like woolly, namby-pamby weakness. What about the macho leaders we all learnt about in school – the Nelsons, Shackletons, Churchills and so on? Well, if you read more about them, you will almost invariably find that the really great leaders succeeded because they inspired genuine affection and respect among their followers. Nelson fought hard to introduce better conditions for his men. Shackleton risked his life to save his expedition team. And Churchill was famously protective of his staff.

None of this is to suggest that you shouldn't be assertive. It is absolutely essential to be able to put forward your point of view and stand up for your own interests. *You will always be more successful if you are polite and friendly.*

This is easy to say, I know, and easy enough to put into practice when things are going well. The difficulties arise when your interests and the interests of the person you're interacting with start to move apart. This is when you start to get angry, or raise your voice.

Think about it! What do you want to get out of the interaction? Why are you talking to this person? It's because you want to achieve something. Now briefly put yourself in their position. Are they likely to be more helpful if you are friendly – or if you are aggressive and rude? Politeness pays!!

Getting to know you...

In his famous book *How to Win Friends and Influence People*, Dale Carnegie wrote: "You can make more friends in two months by becoming interested in other people than you can in two years by trying to get other people interested in you." We briefly glanced at how this works in Chapter 7. Let's look at it in a bit more depth.

Next time you're with a group of friends – in the pub, the office snack room or whatever – have a look around and see who are the more popular people. Is it the ones who never stop talking about themselves, their families and their problems – or the people who don't always say much, but listen and ask questions?

The bottom line is that most people are most interested in themselves. If you can share this interest, they will like you (and probably find you a very interesting person, even if you only ever talk about them!)

Once you accept this simple fact, you can turn it to your advantage in many ways. People who like you are always going to be more willing to help you, or do business with you.

This may seem like an unpleasantly cynical view of relationships – but its redeeming feature is that both sides benefit from it. By showing an interest in them, you may find it easier to persuade the other person to co-operate with you – but they also get a warm glow from your attention!

Salesmen and companies have used this principle for years, and indeed a whole industry of 'Customer Relationship Management' has grown up to help large companies persuade thousands of customers that they are getting personal service. Companies know that if they manage their relationships properly, they will be able to persuade their customers to continue buying their products and not drift off to the competition.

The '**People Folders**' that we have talked about in earlier chapters are your form of Customer Relationship Management. They are where you store the information that lets you demonstrate real interest in the friends and colleagues you interact with every day. They give you a single source of information on the people concerned.

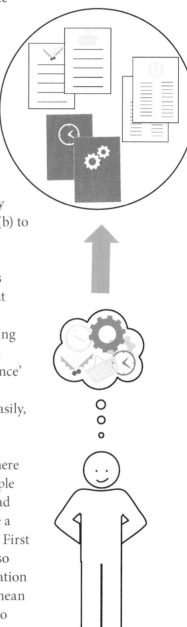

Does this seem unnecessarily complicated, or too 'organised'? Why would you need to have a system, just to remember information about people you like, and maybe see all the time? As always, the answer is because of the limited ability of our memory (a) to retain all the information we need, and (b) to serve it back out at the right time.

Our brains are incredible – they can do things that no computer can even begin to match. But they are not always good at the very simplest tasks. That's why we have shopping lists, packing lists, Christmas card lists – and Terrain Maps and Diaries. We need to get this simple 'reference' information out of our heads and into a place where we know we can access it quickly and easily, when we want it.

People Folders are just the same. They are where we can store what we need to know about People – once again, the clue is in the name. Jane's Dad broke his leg last week; Sophie is going to have a baby in February; Iain has been picked for the First XV; Doug is going on holiday to Iceland; and so on, and so on. All these little scraps of information that mean very little in themselves – but can mean a lot to the person you meet once a month, who will be pleased and impressed by your obvious interest when you ask about them!

'**People Folders**' can take all sorts of forms – not many of them actual folders! Of course, if you are a very organised sort of person, you could keep a 'file' on each of your contacts. Lots of people do, from theatrical agents to secret policemen! But a system like this does tend to get complicated, and time-consuming, and eventually pretty hungry for space.

THERE ARE THREE WAYS YOU MIGHT KEEP FOLDERS:

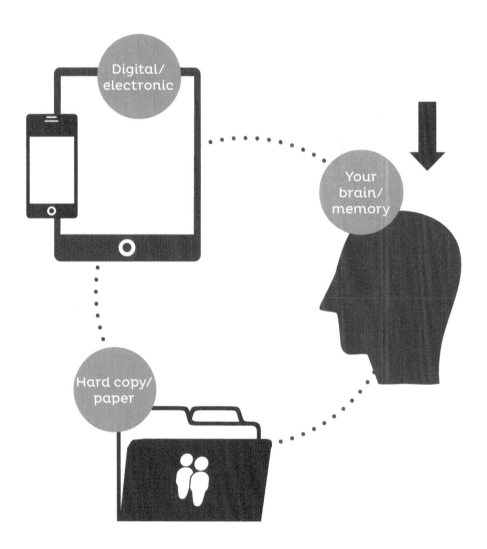

As a relationship develops you will probably find yourself storing information in different locations.

When you first meet someone – your first interaction with them – you learn some things about them and their potential relationship to you. You capture this information during the interaction and then post it to their **People Folder**. Remembering it – storing it in your memory – would be fine if you were sure it would work. But what if you forget their name, company, job title, and contact details? All of this information might be important to you, so you need to keep it in a more reliable place – that is, either on paper or in electronic format.

Name?
Company?
Job Title?

Then, when you next meet or speak to this person you can refer to their **Folder** and make sure that you make best use of the contact. As time goes by and you have more and more interactions with this person, who is becoming increasingly important to you, their **Folder** will grow. By the time they have become your major customer, you will probably be able to rely on your memory to store most of the personal information about them. The business stuff will be kept in hard copy or electronically.

Of course if the customer is really important to your business, you will probably want to back up all of the personal information in your memory to more permanent storage. After all something may happen to you, and someone else in your organisation will need to take over the relationship for you. Your company may already have a system in place to make sure that vital customer information is properly stored and can be retrieved when necessary.

The same principles apply to personal relationships. It's worth making sure that you always store and can recall information about your friends' likes and dislikes, ambitions and dreams – as well as their birthdays and your wedding anniversary! This kind of information means a lot to people, and by showing that it means a lot to you too, you will strengthen your relationships. But you don't need to ensure that your colleagues at work have access to it...!

If you're happiest with something you can touch and scribble on, there are all sorts of card index systems available – from the traditional 'Rolodex' with proper cards (as seen in 1950s Bogart movies!) to Filofax-type systems where you have a page-per-person. Any of these has the advantage of being easy to use, keeping information where you can get your hands on it and add to it fairly quickly and not taking up too much space. The main problem is that they are not always convenient to carry around.

As we noted in Chapter 8, the ideal system for many people is electronic – portable, instantly available and easy to access. We will look at specific applications in the next chapter.

AND AS ALWAYS, REMEMBER THE TWO BASIC RULES:

1 Do not write down something about a person you would be embarrassed for them (or anyone else!) to see.

2 If you wouldn't want someone to write something about you – don't write it about them!

LAWS ON DATA PROTECTION AND FREEDOM OF INFORMATION ARE STRICT: DON'T LEAVE YOURSELF OPEN TO EMBARRASSMENT OR WORSE.

MORE **INTERACTIONS**

Let's look a bit more closely at the interactions
you have with other people. They come in
different forms.

A phone call, e-mail or meeting can be initiated
either by you or by the other person. It can
be informal and unannounced – you contact
them or they contact you without notice, or you
simply meet someone by chance. Or it might
follow an appointment, and have a known
subject or even an agenda.

The dynamics of these interactions can be very
different. It's worth unpicking them a bit, to
see what is the most effective way to handle the
choices you need to make.

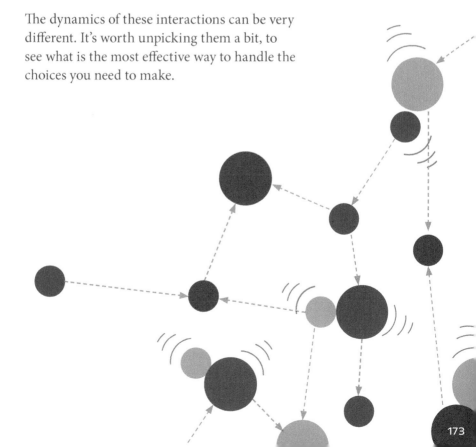

When people contact you without warning

It's always – well, often, at least – good to get a call or visit from someone out of the blue. Sometimes it may be entirely social, and that's great. But most of the time, people have some reason for contacting you. I don't want to sound too cynical about it – but the simple fact is that usually they want something from you, and to some extent they have probably thought about how they are going to get the result they want.

Of course this is far more obvious in a business context: there are few entirely social phonecalls, and certainly no such thing as a free lunch. When Auntie Mary calls, though, even she may well be looking for something – whether it's the recipe for your prize gingerbread or the loan of your lawnmower.

You, on the other hand, have had no prior warning of the event and start off on the back foot. In a social or family situation, this won't matter for 95% of the time – you're probably flattered that Aunt Mary would like your recipe, and delighted to have an excuse not to mow the lawn this weekend. In business, though, you may be in a more difficult position.

In the most basic terms, someone wants something from you – your time, your expertise, some service or product that you can supply. If it's a simple trade enquiry, where you can simply make a sale on normal terms – great! That's business. However, it's quite probable that the person has approached you for some kind of favour – free advice, unpaid help, a discount or whatever.

Now you have a choice: you can help them, or turn them down. Naturally, you don't want to disappoint them – that way you could lose their custom, or at least their goodwill.

If you give them the outcome they want, you will make them happy. Now the dynamics of the interaction are in your favour! You have given them what they want. What do you want from them?

It may be that you just want to bank their goodwill – they will 'owe you one', or perhaps recommend you to their own contacts.

Wherever possible, whenever you are interacting with someone have access to their **People Folder**, in whatever format you keep it. The same goes for **Subject Folders**, but the key difference is that while with a **Subject Folder** it is perfectly acceptable to be seen checking its contents, with **People Folders** it's not so easy! If you're on the phone, the other person will not see you accessing their **People Folder**, but in a face to face meeting it could obviously be embarrassing. The only thing to do is practise – plan as much as possible, improve your memory, if necessary rehearse and visualise how you expect the meeting to go. Learn from top sales people – try to develop genuine empathy and improve your communications skills.

If you know that you would like something specific in exchange for your favour (maybe a glance at your '**People Folder**' will help!) your immediate action will depend on several factors. How generous was your help – just how happy have you made them? Do you – and they – have time for any discussion necessary? How long will it be before you see them again?

The main point to bear in mind is that, human nature being what it is, their gratitude for your helpfulness will fade remarkably quickly!

All things being equal, it is usually best to strike while the iron is hot!

Contacting other people without warning

Of course if you are the one making the initial contact, the positions are reversed.

You are making contact for a reason – you want something, or have some sort of aim in mind. You also have the time and opportunity to plan how you want to handle the meeting. Your **People Folder** will make sure that you remember all you need to know about your previous contact with the other person. If what you want is important, you also have time to Visualise and Mentally Rehearse your contact.

If you are successful and achieve the outcome you hoped for, it is now time for you to be ready to show your gratitude to your benefactor. They might be happy to accept your thanks, and store your goodwill – or they might ask for something specific in return. Either way, be generous! If you keep taking without giving something back, this will soon become obvious and you may find your contacts being less forthcoming.

The best case, in virtually any interaction, is that both parties go away afterwards feeling pleased with the outcome. Making people happy is a two-way street!

Meetings set up in advance

These can range from a cup of coffee in a snack bar to a formal meeting of a company board. What they have in common is that all the participants are aware of who will be attending, and probably exactly what business will be discussed. (For a formal meeting, an agenda should have been issued, even if only an e-mailed outline of what's to be covered.)

Everyone therefore has ample time to decide what they want to get out of the meeting, and how they expect to achieve it. If the meeting is a simple business/social one-on-one, there will probably be very few business topics, and these may be almost engulfed by social chat.

Formal 'business' meetings – whether of the board of Sainsbury's or just the committee of the tennis club – will have an agenda setting out exactly what is to be discussed and decided. Any social chitchat will be confined to breaks in the meeting.

If you have particular objectives you want to attain in formal meetings, you may well want to do some Visualisation and Mental Rehearsal beforehand. Be warned, though – especially in bigger meetings with many participants, you may need an intensive course in Game Theory to predict just how the meeting will unroll as demands are made, and alliances form and break up!

Very often the best tactic is to choose and concentrate on just one important outcome you would like to achieve, and go for that. As in any other negotiation, you will have to be prepared to argue your case – and also probably to make some concessions along the way. And the same rule applies here as in most human interactions – it pays to show your gratitude for concessions and favours given to you. It may be your turn next time!

> In all of these interactions – formal or informal, planned or not – try to remember your overall goals. Everything you do, all of the outcomes you seek, should be small steps on the way to achieving your goals – and ultimately, your **North Pole Goal**. If they are not – you're going the wrong way!

How do interactions fit in with your Terrain Map?

As we saw in Chapter 6, unplanned interruptions – phone calls, emails, casual meetings – can play havoc with the smooth-flowing day that you may have set out in your Terrain Map. There's nothing like life for making things complicated!

The basic rules to keep some sort of order are:

→ always be conscious of where you are on your Terrain Map
→ try to ensure that whatever you do brings you closer to achieving your goals
→ If you follow these, you will ensure that you can stay focused on the interaction in progress, aware of what your preferred outcomes are and with a good idea of how it's going to affect your day as set out in your Terrain Map.
→ How much time can you allow for this interaction?
→ If it overshoots, what is the cost to you in terms of other places you are supposed to be, and things you should be doing?

When you have answered these questions you can work out whether you are willing to pay the price, and how you will handle the changes to your plans.

This probably sounds like a complex and cumbersome set of questions and answers in response to a simple event! But of course you don't need to sit down and ponder it all – as with so much of the **TRIM** system, once you are able to apply the basic principles all of the calculations happen almost automatically. It's really a case of always having a good idea in your head of where you are in your day, what you should be doing and – importantly – what comes next.

The Key Steps

There are three Key Steps to doing all of this:

1 Have instant access to your various **People** and **Subject Folders** (however you keep them), so that you can quickly locate the information you need about the people you meet and the tasks you are engaged in.

2 Capture all the relevant information and actions that arise from meetings and activities. (Your interactions.)

3 Then post them making sure that everything is stored in the right places.

Always post new information to the relevant **Folders** as soon as possible – the sooner the better as while updating you will probably remember bits and pieces that you might otherwise have completely forgotten. Additionally, if you wait too long to post the information, any untidy scribbles and cryptic notes may be impossible to decipher!

Also always check that you're using your opportunities to your advantage in achieving your goals as easily and effectively as possible

Once you're used to following these three basic steps, it's just a circular process:

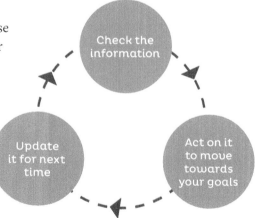

WHAT COULD BE MORE SIMPLE....?

INFORMATION

Following up on Interactions

Have another look at the 'Interactions' picture below. As you can see, interactions produce results in either or both of two main categories:

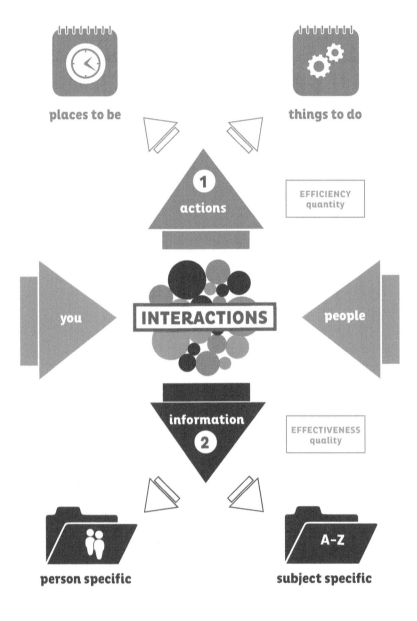

Many interactions will have elements covering all of these. To maximise your personal effectiveness and efficiency you need to make sure that they are all captured, stored in the right place and then dealt with at the right time and in the right way.

Things to Do will normally be transferred to your Terrain Maps, if they are within that timescale, or else to your **Things to Do** diary.

Places to Be will also go to the Terrain Maps if that's appropriate, and always to the **Places to Be** diary to avoid double-booking.

Information, about **People** or **Subjects**, needs to be recorded while it is fresh in your mind. You can't record everything: even if you could, you would end up with so much information that it would be almost impossible to process or recover. Some will be factual ('Kevin won't be attending the Board Meeting next Friday') and some may be subjective ('...and from the tone of his voice, Kevin is about to be fired from the Board anyway!')

As you are entering your information, you will probably find that you remember additional points that add depth and meaning to the simple facts – and you may well notice links or patterns emerging.

The information that you are recording will often be relevant to many 'folders' at the same time: for example **People**, **Places to Be** and **Subjects**. Unless you have a great cross-referencing system, you should add the information to as many folders as you feel are relevant. The only rules are that everything should be easily found.

You need the information, and you need it now! There's no point knowing that it is neatly filed in a notebook on your desk, if you're just about to go into the meeting...

easily found

up to date

easily accessible

Once again, you may be thinking that I am trying to turn you into some sort of filing clerk, spending your whole life obsessively recording information in a huge stack of ledgers, diaries and folders. I promise you it's not like that! I'm using the expressions 'diaries' and 'folders' just to remind you that there are different kinds of information that you need to store, and be able to find again when you need it.

This doesn't mean that you actually need to have separate physical places to store these different items. You may feel quite happy writing them all down in one large notebook or diary – though I think you will find it easier to have at least a separate section for your notes on people, and maybe one for the various projects you might have going on.

Of course, the ultimate way of storing all your information in one easily-accessible place is to use the power of your smartphone, tablet or desktop computer – or, ideally, all three. We'll look at how this works in the next chapter.

But it's up to you! As long as you are confident that you can store the information you need, and find it again when you want to use it, that is absolutely all that's called for. As with most elements of **TRIM**, what is right for you and your lifestyle is what you should use.

MANAGEMENT

Management is the art of getting things done. However, here are two definitions of 'management' which we might use in the **TRIM** context:

> Management is getting more out of people than they would otherwise give – preferably without them noticing or objecting

> Management is getting other people to act in a way that advances your own ability to achieve your personal goals

In the work context, it is almost inevitable that your aims and goals will depend to some extent on the success of your organisation – so (even if you were not being paid to do so!) it's in your best interest to make it work as well as possible. People will normally work harder to achieve their own goals than those of their employer – so if you're in a position to do so, it makes sense to ensure that the goals of the organisation are as much as possible in line with those of the individuals working for it. This includes you!

Management styles change, and different techniques might work well in different situations. Genghis Khan and Mahatma Ghandi were both superb leaders and managers, but they clearly didn't go to the same management training school!

Nevertheless, they both achieved great success by making sure that their followers shared the same goals as they did.

Nagging

As you know, the central principle of The **TRIM** Course is to ensure that you always deliver on your promises, on time and to the quality required.

Unfortunately, most of the world has not yet benefited from The **TRIM** Course! If you are relying on other people to deliver the inputs that you need to help you achieve your goals, you may have to decide how to ensure that they come up with the goods.

You have two basic choices: you can simply trust them to deliver, or you can recontact them to remind them of their commitments to you.

Obviously, trusting them to deliver is best: it doesn't waste your time (or theirs), and they may well deliver to a higher standard than if you are breathing down their neck. A great deal will depend on how well you know them, and your past experiences of their work. You will also need to decide how critical their input is – what the 'cost' to you will be if they don't deliver.

If you don't know the person, and really need them to produce on time, you may have no choice but to remind them and check on progress. You may then get what you need, when you need it – but there are disadvantages. The person you are chasing may resent being 'nagged' – especially if they had every intention of delivering on time anyway. This could lead to a lower quality of work than you might have received. And of course, you will have to spend precious time and effort on your follow-ups.

However, there is a third way. If you note the other person's commitment to you in their **People Folder**, then you can choose an appropriate moment to drop a subtle reminder into a conversation, without putting any pressure on them. If you do this properly, the recipient of the reminder will not resent it and might even appreciate your interest and reminder. (Who knows, they may have actually forgotten their promise to you!).

TIME

I've left 'Time' to last because there isn't really much to say about it, except that as we have noted before, the idea of 'managing' it is a bit of a daydream! Time is time: we all know how quickly it moves, and we all get the same number of hours each day. We can't buy it, or borrow it, or save it up for later.

More to the point, time is of course essential to anything you do in the other areas of Relationships, Information and Management – they all rely on our appreciation of time, and the limitations it puts on us.

So why are bookshops stuffed with books about 'Time Management'? What they and innumerable courses try to teach are ways of using our available time as efficiently and effectively as possible.

A fine ambition. However, as you will by now have realised, The **TRIM** Course is based on the recognition that as well as regulating the way we use our time, we also need to tend our relationships and the information we process every minute of every day.

How time is allocated is a critical part of the **TRIM** system. **TRIM's** two main tools, the **Weekly Helicopter Trip** and Terrain Maps, both have time as their baseline. But everything in **TRIM** is designed to take full account of the value of Relationships, and the vital role of Information and Management, in everything we do.

Ink or Electrons?

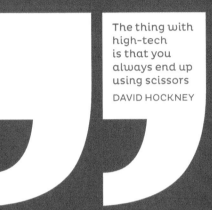

The thing with
high-tech
is that you
always end up
using scissors
DAVID HOCKNEY

Everyone would like to be more efficient and effective in the way that they organise their lives – but understandably enough, nobody wants to spend lots of time on the mechanics of actually doing the organising!

So one of the most common queries I've had from students is:

> I'm a busy person, and the reason I came along to the **TRIM** course is to make my life easier. But now you want me to spend half my day filling in **People Folders**, **Things-to-Do Folders**, **Places-to-Be** diaries, **Things-to-Do** diaries, **Terrain Maps**.... I haven't got time to be a filing clerk on top of everything else!

Well, here's the good news: of course, you don't need to. In this chapter we'll look at the ways in which computers, the Internet and mobile phone technology have transformed our ability to store and retrieve the information we need – wherever we are.

WHAT WOULD WE LIKE OUR COMPUTERS TO DO?

PROS AND CONS

WHAT'S AVAILABLE

WHICH TO CHOOSE?

WHAT NEXT?

But first a health warning! Trying to write anything about information technology, in its various and mutating forms, is like trying to describe an explosion: you can give the general picture, but the individual bits change too fast to explain. So what follows is an impression of the world as it is at the moment, and as I see it developing over the next while – but it is always possible that some completely new piece of technology or software will come over the horizon at any time and change the whole game. What I'm trying to do here is just give you an idea of how the bits fit together, so that at least you can follow what's happening!

I should also say that I don't claim any computer expertise for myself! Like most people, I prefer just to press the keys and let the experts work out the complicated bits. If you're a whiz with computers you probably know all this stuff already. This chapter is written for computer dummies like me!

WHAT WOULD WE LIKE OUR COMPUTERS TO DO?

Let's go back to basics for a moment. Think about what you have learned so far. In a nutshell, you need to be in the right place, at the right time, with the relevant and correct information to hand.

➜ know where you should be

➜ know where you need to be next, and at what time

➜ make sure you always know what's the best thing you can be doing with your time, at that time, all of the time

➜ keep tabs on all of the other things that you need to do, and places you will need to be later

➜ have instant access to information about people you interact with **(People Folders)**

➜ have instant access to information about subjects you are working on and/or discussing **(Subject Folders)**

➜ be able to capture/record new information and actions that arise from your interactions

➜ be able to transfer/post the information and actions to the correct place for future instant access

The first three 'musts' – knowing where you should be, where you need to be next and the best thing for you to do – are taken care of by your Terrain Maps. Where do the Terrain Maps come from? As you now know, each Map is built up over a number of days, using information drawn from your **Places-to-Be** and **Things-to-Do** diaries. They are the essential sources of information that you use during your **Weekly Helicopter Trip** to provide the basic skeletons of your Terrain Maps – though you will fill up and add more detail to the Maps as the day to which they refer gets closer, as well as throughout the day in question.

These two diaries also provide longer-term information about tasks that you have to do, and places you will need to be, further ahead than your current Terrain Maps. In due course this information will be used for a **Weekly Helicopter Trip**, and it will eventually make its way onto Terrain Maps for some time in the future.

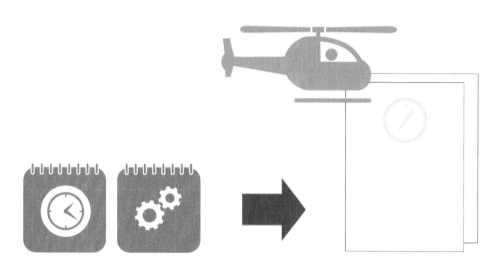

You need different information about the people you interact with. If a meeting or phonecall has been planned well in advance, you will have time to look in the appropriate '**People Folder**' to check whether there are any particular subjects to ask about – or topics to avoid! If you have the information available and can access it quickly, you may be able to do the same even if the person phones you unexpectedly. For chance encounters, of course, you will probably still have to rely on your memory! But in any of these cases, you need to be able to record the outcomes – information and actions – from the interaction, and then post/transfer to the correct places.

So far, to make the workings of the system clearer we've talked about the various folders and diaries as physically separate items – with a book, or a set of folders or filing cards for each. But although it's essential to understand that each of these has a unique function, holding different kinds of information, in the real world it would be cumbersome and impractical to carry them around or even give them desk space.

Enter the computer, riding a white horse.

Today virtually everyone has access to a computer, more than two-thirds of UK mobile phone users have smartphones and 'tablet computers' such as the iPad are commonplace. We are inseparable from our mobile phones: given the choice of losing their wallets or their mobiles, 30% of the people surveyed chose to keep their phones.

Hanna Marin, in the US TV show 'Pretty Little Liars', summed it up pretty well: "I can't go around without a phone. That's like going around without a brain!"

And the trend can only increase...

This instant, almost universal access to computers revolutionises the way that we can apply **TRIM** principles and use the **TRIM** tools.

But the beauty of computer-based systems is the ease with which these various items can be integrated and made to work together.

"But what of Terrain Maps?" I hear you cry! Ah...well, the honest answer is that I have not yet found a really satisfactory way of transferring my Terrain Maps away from ink to electrons. Later in this chapter I'll look at a couple of possibilities – but until someone invents a screen that I can really scribble on, I think I'll be sticking to paper.

PROS AND CONS

Before you pitch in to the latest supercool app promising to double your productivity with twice the fun and three times the rewards, let's just have a quick glance at the pros and cons of letting a computer tell you how to run your life.

The massive advantage, as we have seen, is the ability to carry all of your essential information with you so that it is available everywhere, at any time. With the right program on the right device, it's all there. What's not to like?

Well...you need to be aware that many internet-based programs don't actually live on your phone or computer. So just at the moment when you desperately need to remember the name of your sister's new boyfriend

→ your phone tells you that it has 'No Service'
→ the new operating system has rearranged all your contacts, and
→ your battery dies

... and all this before you lose your phone!

We all know from painful experience that electronics are, basically, not always on our side. Most devices seem to have a built-in stress detection circuit which ensures that they will work perfectly well until we really, really need them. There's not much you can do about this – and the huge advantages of using smartphone and computer facilities mean that we're not about to ditch them and go back to paper. But it's worthwhile remembering that you can't always rely on them to behave properly, and whenever you can, leave yourself enough time and mental energy to play their little games!

The other great advantage of technology is that it not only allows you to retrieve information quickly and easily (if it's in a good mood....) but also ensures that you can store stuff at the earliest possible opportunity. So instead of trying to decipher scribbled notes hours after your meeting, you can enter all the relevant details straight into the right places.

Devices like smart phones, tablets and desktops increasingly use 'the cloud' to store data and even programs. This just means that data doesn't stay on the machine you're using, but is stored on a huge worldwide network of computers so that it's always protected even if your own machine breaks down or gets lost. This 'automatic backup' is obviously a good safety feature: the last thing you want is for all of your information to disappear for ever when you drop your smartphone in the bath. But even better, it means that your data can be shared automatically between several devices. If you have a smartphone, a tablet computer and a desktop, you want to be able to work at any of them. Cloud computing means that your essential information – contacts, calendar, task list and so on – is always available and synchronised to all your machines.

Once again, these advantages depend on a good internet connection and properly functioning programs. If you live and work in an area with good connectivity and are familiar with the programs you're using, then you will probably have few problems. Nevertheless, it is always worth bearing in mind that things can go wrong and planning accordingly!

WHAT'S AVAILABLE?

There are literally hundreds of apps for smart phones and tablets which help to alphabetize, categorise, prioritise and generally organise our time, tasks and contacts. Desktop computers give access to sophisticated 'office suites' and Customer Relationship Management programs. It's a maze, and it would be very easy to spend a lot of money for software with capabilities far beyond the needs of most individuals. When you are deciding which might be right for you, I suggest that you remember the basic foundation of **TRIM** as summed up in the Interactions graphic – all you want your system to do is

ORGANISE YOUR INFORMATION SO THAT IT'S THERE WHEN YOU NEED TO TAKE ACTIONS!

Because there are so many apps and programs available, with new ones arriving every week and old ones disappearing like snow off a wall, I am not going to review specialised software which claims to organise your contacts by the colour of their eyes, or provide a calendar for the next thousand years, or whatever. These are all out there, and they are great fun, and occasionally they might be useful. But none of them provides the kind of overall, integrated view that we ideally want to keep our lives in order and running smoothly.

In this chapter I am going to look briefly at three of the best-known integrated programs. They have all been around for some time, and because they are provided by some of the biggest companies in the world there's a good chance that they will survive and continue to get better as time goes on.

MICROSOFT OFFICE

Microsoft has been producing business software for longer than almost everyone, and over the years many of the most popular individual programs have been integrated into 'suites'. The best known is Microsoft Office. The basic version includes word processing, email, diary, spreadsheet and presentation software, and more elaborate (and expensive) options include powerful database, desktop publishing, information sharing and collaboration programs.

All of these are interlinked so that appointments in the calendar can automatically generate tasks ('**Things to Do**'), emails can be incorporated into presentations, and so on. The highest level 'Enterprise' version of Office is powerful enough to run a small country – with a price tag to match.

However, more basic versions are often 'bundled' at very reasonable cost with new desktop and laptop computers – and these provide quite enough capability for our purposes. Alternatively, Microsoft offers 'Office 365' – an online version of the suite which currently (early 2014) costs around £8 per month. This gives access to virtually all of the 'enterprise' software and around 20GB of 'cloud based' storage. It also enables up to 4 members of the same family to share the software and have access to calendars – which can be handy for co-ordinating the family diaries.

SOFTWARE CALENDARS

Within Microsoft Office, the most important program for **TRIM** purposes is Outlook. Outlook effectively provides Contacts ('**People folders**') and Calendars ('**Places to Be**' diaries) linked in to Task Lists ('**Things to Do**' diaries). There are then any number of ways of keeping your '**Subject Folders**' – in the form of Microsoft Word documents, Excel spreadsheets or even Access databases. However, if you have one of the more fully-featured versions of Office – or if you use Office 365, the online version – then you will be able to use Microsoft OneNote.

Finally, because Outlook is mainly designed for desktop computers, you will need a way of accessing and working with your information from a mobile phone or tablet. As I'll explain this can be done in various ways. It's not necessary if you subscribe to Office 365, which is already set up to talk to most mobile devices.

I'll look briefly at each of these components.

Outlook

Outlook started off as mainly as an email system, and for many people that remains its main function. As you might expect, it does it well and there are plenty of bells and whistles. You can set the program up exactly to suit your own requirements, with multiple accounts and subaccounts, rules to direct mail from different senders to different files and so on. Importantly, Outlook contains an extremely effective anti-spam filter which is automatically updated to keep your inboxes clear of junk mail.

For **TRIM** purposes, however, the most important parts of Outlook are its Contacts and Calendar functions, and its Task List.

Contacts

Like any other contact list, Outlook Contacts allows you to enter huge amounts of detail about your contacts – everything from their holiday home phone number to their cat's inside leg measurement. How much you actually choose to keep for each contact is up to you! For some business colleagues you might want quite a bit – their mobile number, alternative email addresses, the name of their PA, their photo, and so on. For ephemeral business contacts – the man who is painting your window frames, or the garage where you left your car for repair – just a name and a phone number may be fine.

In either case, any good Contacts program ensures that you always have a permanent, instantly-accessible record of who you know and might need to communicate with. It will also be searchable, and when you have it on your phone, it will automatically dial the right number for you.

So much for the basics of recording contact details. Where electronic contact lists really start showing their **TRIM** worth, though, is in enabling you to make notes about each contact. Outlook Contacts are particularly good for this. Each contact page includes a large area which you can use, effectively, for any purpose you like. So you can record each meeting with a contact, arrange items into groups, put in dates, comments, reminders – in fact, anything you might want to put in your 'People Folder', with the advantage that all of this information is searchable. When you vaguely remember that someone said they were going to Paris in October – Outlook will find the right note for you.

OCTOBER

27

You can also have several different Contact lists – for work, friends, sport or whatever. This is most useful when you want to share access to friends in one particular area, but not all. Of course you can combine them all when you are looking for one contact but can't remember which list you put them in!

Calendar

Outlook's Calendar, like everything else in Office, is almost infinitely customisable. You can enter 'Places to Be' with options for reminders from two weeks to ten minutes beforehand, have different colours for events in different categories, set up meetings and group schedules, and share your calendar with other people – though Outlook isn't as good at this as some others, unless you are using Office 365. You can also set up 'recurrent' appointments – so if you go to an evening class every Wednesday at 6.15, you don't need to enter it into the Calendar over and over again.

The 'new appointment' screen also contains a large area for Notes, so you can add key points and reminders for meetings, preparations you need to make before the appointment, and references to other items that might be useful. Although Calendars are not as flexible as Contacts or Tasks in what you can add into the Notes section – for example, you can't put in clickable links or email addresses – there is a facility for attaching files, so you can add in documents which you might need for background reading.

And of course, you can use the Notes area during and after the meeting to record decisions, actions you will need to take and future engagements – so that you can easily cut and paste these to the right locations later.

As with Contacts, you can have as many different Calendars as you like – for personal, work, people's birthdays, or whatever – and you can merge them or display them side by side. Although Outlook is not great at sharing Calendar information, there are ways of doing it – and many other applications can synchronise their own Calendars with your Outlook one, ensuring that both are kept up to date without having to make separate entries.

Tasks

Outlook has two ways of noting what you have to do. It distinguishes between 'Tasks', which are items you create in Outlook to track until you have completed them, and 'To-Do items' which can be any Outlook item – an email, a Task or a Contact – that you have 'flagged' for follow-up. 'Flagging' simply means clicking on a little symbol in the heading of the item, which creates a 'flag' which remains in place until you tell it to go away: you can create different colours of flags to indicate how urgently the item needs attention, or set the number of days it will wait.

To create a Task you use a form, as for Contacts and Calendar Appointments. You can give the Task a title, a start date and a due date, assign it to a category and then indicate its priority, status (not started/in progress/waiting for someone else) and what percentage of the task is completed. Importantly for the **TRIM** techniques, you can also mark when you need to follow-up.

This process is ideal for setting up major tasks where you need to be able to monitor progress, maybe assign parts of it to other people, and associate with other tasks. Once again there is a large 'Notes' section into which you can put other items such as documents, links and so on, and write yourself notes about the task or project concerned.

'Flagging' is a much simpler process which just notes that a diary item, email or contact needs to be followed up. When you click the 'flag' symbol at the side of the screen the flag changes colour, and in most screens you have the option of setting different flags to show the urgency of the follow-up – or even setting a reminder before the due time. This is a great 'quick and dirty' way of noting that you need to take action on something – even if this is simply to extract information or post it elsewhere.

Every item that you flag will now appear in your 'To-Do- list', which you can put at the right-hand side or at the bottom of your email or calendar windows – so that it's always visible.

And putting them all together...

As you are probably beginning to realise, when you put together your calendar, contacts, task and to-do lists on one page, you are getting pretty close to having Outlook create an on-screen Terrain Map!

This is what Tim's Outlook page might look like.

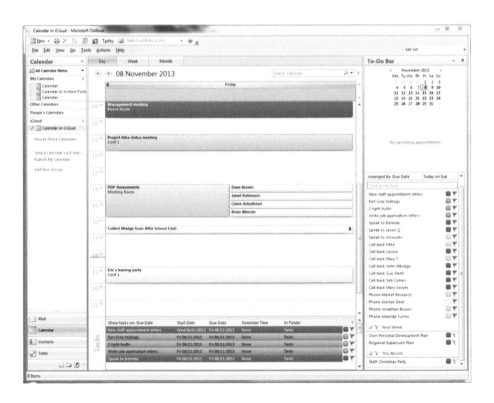

As Tim goes through his day, he can double-click on each item to read notes that he may have made beforehand, and afterwards add to these notes or open the appropriate folder straight away to update information. He can open the contact 'folder' for anyone he will be speaking to, which will also give him their phone number. His appointments and 'to-do's' are all coloured to show which category they belong to – personal, management, family, social and so on.

He can mark 'one-off' tasks like returning phone calls or speaking to individuals as 'completed' just by clicking the flag beside them. For more complex or longer-term jobs like the Regional Development Plan, his own Personal Development Plan or planning the Staff Christmas Party, he can open the Task Sheet and note progress, next steps, critical dates and any other relevant information.

As we saw in Chapter 6, Tim's day actually developed in a few unpredictable ways – a meeting had to be put back by half an hour, he had an unexpected lunchtime visitor and so on. By using Outlook he would be able to make changes 'on the fly' to his appointments, quickly look at his notes on people in his Contacts folder and amend tasks and '**Things to Do**' as they developed.

Finally, if he also used MicroSoft's OneNote program, which is also part of the Office suite, he would be able to pull together all the information on his meetings and major tasks in one place. OneNote provides a simple way of collecting emails, contact details, documents, web links, photographs, diagrams, drafts and notes in one place. It's a bit like having a big project file, except that OneNote does the filing – you just need to tell it what you want in there. Everything is searchable, and you can group and stack all kinds of different items exactly as you want to and then pull them out at will. OneNote is a very powerful tool for turning a disorganised mass of information into a useful resource!

So what's not to like?

As I hope I've shown, MS Office is a superbly integrated suite of scheduling and information handling applications which can get very near the target of 'digital **TRIM**'. So if Office is so good at organising our lives, why don't we all use it? Well, there are a few drawbacks...

First of all, the Office software suite is really designed for use on a desktop computer – and preferably one in a large office environment, with a central server handling mail, calendars and so on. The versions for home and small-office use are fine but do lack some of the more powerful features (though the version available to students is very favourably priced and contains everything).

Of course Office runs perfectly well on a laptop, and indeed on a tablet using a Microsoft Windows operating system – but Microsoft has so far (early 2014) refused to release a full version to run on iPad or Android tablets or smartphones. There are many apps available which will open, run and allow editing of Office files – but so far I have not found any which provide the same level of integration of the different functions. Most of the apps on offer are pretty dire, and (as I have discovered!) you can spend a long time learning to drive them before discovering that they really don't do the job.

So, if you are able to run your life from a laptop or Windows tablet, Office may well be the best software to provide your digital TRIM.

If you have Office on your home desktop, you will probably find that you use it in any case to store and process most of the information in your Calendar, Contacts and Task List. But, as I'll describe below, you will probably also use different apps on a portable device – a smartphone and/or a tablet – to retrieve the information for you to use on the move.

Google Apps   **GOOGLE APPS**

Google is almost the exact opposite of Microsoft, in that everything in the Google world has always been designed to run remotely, rather than on a corporate network or desktop computer.

As everyone knows, Google started off as a search engine so efficient that it blew away most of its competitors and added a new word to languages worldwide: "I Googled it...." But then Google email – Gmail – arrived, as a free, Internet-based system with loads of free storage in 'the Cloud'. In other words, data didn't take up space on your own computer's hard disk, but was stored on Google's servers anywhere in the world. This not only meant that you could access your stuff from any Internet-enabled machine, anywhere in the world, but that everything was automatically backed-up so that it didn't get lost when your beloved two-year-old poured orange juice all over your computer.

Not surprisingly, Gmail was immediately popular (as was Microsoft's equivalent, Hotmail). Google then went on to add more and more applications, which all link together – some better than others! Now as well as Gmail you can have calendars, contacts and tasks – as well as word processing, note-taking and numerous other apps. All are free for personal or small-business users.

Google Calendar and Contacts offer broadly the same facilities as Office: you can tailor entries on your Calendar with different colours, reminders and so on, set repeats, alarms and reminders, and invite other contacts. If you enter the location of the event, by postcode, street or business name, you can then click on it to see a map and get directions, or see a photograph in Google Street View.

Google's Contacts allow you to enter all of the standard elements of contact details, with a Notes field which you can use to keep track of all the information you would normally post to your 'Person Folders'. It is possible to synchronise Google Contacts with mobile devices using iOS (iPhones and iPads) or Android operating systems, though setting this up is a little complicated. You can import all of your Contacts and Calendar information from Outlook or most other programs, so you don't have to start from scratch – but once you have decided to go with Google, you really need to be consistent and use Google apps for all your Calendar, Contact and Task List information. Though you can – at least in theory – set up synchronising with desktop programs, it's not easy and there's plenty of scope for information to fall through the cracks!

One drawback is that Contacts and the Task List are only visible from the Gmail window – so it's sometimes necessary to have two windows open, and new tasks don't currently (early 2014) seem to be automatically added to the Calendar – though they were in an earlier version. As mentioned before, all of the main providers are constantly developing their offerings and it is impossible to give definitive guidance! Most of the developments are welcome improvements, but not all!

It's not possible (at least, not yet!) to get Google apps to produce a page that looks like a Terrain Map as I described it in Chapter 5. But in practice, I don't think this is too serious: the main point is that on your internet-enabled desktop computer, your smartphone and your tablet you have integrated access to your calendar, contacts and to-do list – with the added bonus of instant click-through access to maps. Google also makes it easy to share Calendars, and indeed Contacts if you want to – so it's simple to keep a family Calendar up to date with everyone's activities.

The illustration on the right shows the Google version of how Tim's diary might look on 8 November 2013. As you can see, all of his main appointments are noted with times and venues. By clicking on any of them, he could see further notes of what he will be doing – and he could insert links into these to take him to documents, graphics or contact details. Google Maps are also completely integrated, so – since all of this is available on his smartphone or tablet as well as his desktop – he never needs to get lost on the way to a meeting.

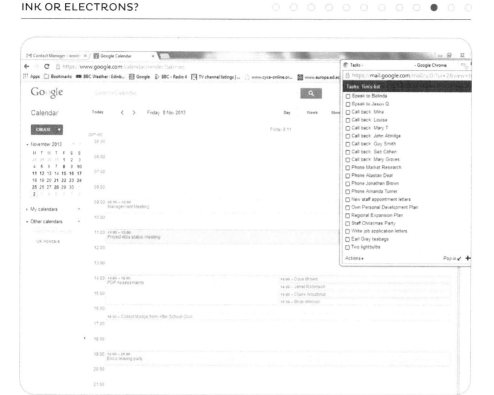

The obvious problem with Google apps is that you might not have full access to them all if you don't have a solid internet connection. This is potentially a real show-stopper, and Google has realised this. In fact, it is possible to enable Gmail, Contacts and Calendar to work 'offline'. This involves loading data onto your mobile device rather than leaving it all in 'the Cloud', so that you can work with the apps when you don't have wi-fi or a good phone data connection. You're obviously restricted in what you can do, but everything is restored and messages, appointments and so on are quickly updated when you re-connect.

Of course the other great advantage of using Google apps is that it is completely free!

I have found that it takes a little while to get used to the Google way of doing things, but when you do, everything is well-integrated and works very well. It's not quite as slick as Microsoft Outlook, and things certainly slow down with a poor Internet connection. But as a form of Digital **TRIM**, it gives you everything you need at no cost.

Well worth a look!

APPLE

Apple has always been renowned for producing superbly user-friendly desktop and laptop computers, which can run beautifully designed software packages including Microsoft Office. However, what makes Apple particularly relevant to Digital **TRIM** are the iPhone and iPad. These devices have revolutionised the way that we regard mobile computing, in effect turning the phone in our pocket into a fully-featured computer – as well as a GPS mapping device and, of course, a portable stereo system, TV and camera. And, with literally hundreds of thousands of apps available, virtually anything else we want it to be...

The Apple world is now built around the iCloud, Apple's Internet-based storage and sharing system. Apple has tried hard to ensure that all of its devices are fully integrated, and that its own software is capable of talking to others – importantly, including Microsoft Windows programs like Outlook.

This means that the Calendar, Contacts and Task List (which Apple calls 'Reminders') can all be synchronised across all of the devices – desktop, iPhone and iPad. Information can be accessed and updated on any of them and is immediately available on all three. All have a 'notes' facility, and although some of the interfaces are not as configurable as Outlook or Google they are amazingly well integrated, both with each other and with external programs. For example, if you receive an email with an invitation in it, it is simple with one tap to check whether you are free at that time: and if you want to add the event to your Calendar you can do so, with mapping information derived from the address and other details taken from Contacts.

The following images show Apple's calendar and task list. They really can't give a very accurate idea of the capability of the Apple system, which mainly depends on the ability to 'click through' from any item to its details and description.

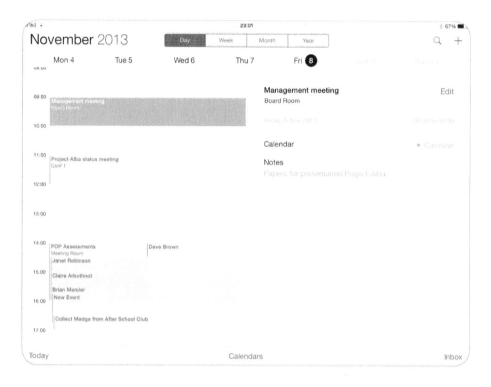

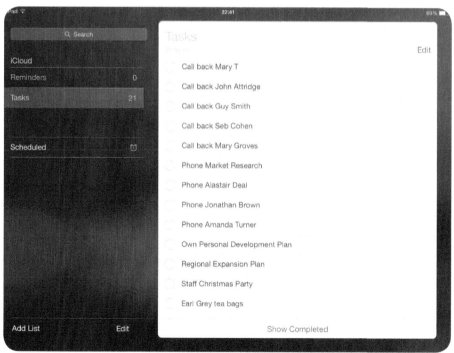

One of Apple's most entertaining abilities is to set a 'Location-based Reminder'. If you set a reminder on your iPhone you have the option of telling the phone to activate the Reminder – normally by playing a sound – when you reach a specific location. If you use Siri, the voice-operated command system, you can give your instructions simply be talking to the phone: "When I get home, remind me to feed the cat." The phone's GPS will detect when you arrive at your house, and your phone will ping to show you a message saying 'Feed the cat'. Sounds like a clever gimmick? Maybe – but it's also an incredibly useful way of quickly making a note to do something.

All of the above is based on the Apple system, but Android phones and tablets also have access to a huge number of apps, and most of the Apple functionality is available at very little cost.

WHICH TO CHOOSE?

As I hope you have gathered from the descriptions above, there is a wide variety of software programs and apps available to help digitise the **TRIM** tools and techniques. Most people I know use a mixture of different hardware and software to put together a system that suits their own needs and abilities. If you are a wizard with computers you may decide to put together your own selection of programs and apps, using their advanced settings to make sure that they work well together and do what you want.

For most of us, already staggering under an avalanche of techno-speak and probably struggling with an out-of–date computer and years of accumulated data, the answer is bound to be a compromise between what we feel we need to simplify life rather than complicate it, what we reckon we can manage to put together, and what we can afford.

There is no need to make a huge leap from paper to the very newest, shiniest software offerings – it is quite possible to make a step-by-step transition as it suits you and as you begin to be familiar with what is available.

As always, you should do whatever suits you best. Don't feel pressured into using the technology just because it is there!

What is important is to remember the basic principles of **TRIM**! The software won't do everything for you: you still need to choose the information that you store, and the way you allocate your time and abilities. Modern devices – computers, smartphones and tablets – simply make it easier to monitor how your day is progressing, to store and access the information you need, and to ensure that you manage your time and information as effectively as possible.

Technology can make things easier, but it can't solve the most fundamental problems. A car will allow you to travel long distances very quickly – but you still need to decide where you want to get to, and the route you're going to use to arrive there. In just the same way, computers and smartphones will help with the mechanics of life, but they can't define your goals, or tell you how to achieve them.

Most important of all, even the cleverest screens won't manage what is at the heart of everything to do with **TRIM** – your interactions with family, friends and colleagues. Only you can do that – and the relationships you create and maintain will decide how successful, how happy, and how valued you are.

And finally....

You may remember that when we looked at Terrain Maps in Chapter 5 I said that for me, nothing beat a paper copy that I could scribble on, scratch things out on, doodle in and finally scrumple up and throw at the cat. I still stick to this – though the great advantage of having all my information at my fingertips may eventually convert me! But there is a half-way stage: it is of course quite possible to take a print-out of the Office page containing the day's Calendar and Tasks, and use this as a Terrain Map to carry round and write on. This provides some of the advantages – particularly the fact that it is produced more or less automatically as I enter details of appointments and tasks. However, it also misses out on many of the best features of a fully digital system: the main one is the ability constantly to amend and update information throughout the system, more or less in real time.

It's up to you!

FREEDOM OF CHOICE

WHAT NEXT?

As I said at the beginning of the chapter, all of the above describes what is available now, and how we can use it to put the **TRIM** tools and techniques into practice.

I deliberately haven't opened the Pandora's Box of social media - Facebook, Twitter and so on – partly because I don't fully understand it myself, partly because it's still developing so quickly that it's difficult to get a handle on it, and partly because it's difficult to see just how it fits into **TRIM**. Certainly people will use social media to help organise their lives – many already run almost their entire social scene using Facebook, and new applications for Twitter seem to arrive almost daily. What you need to remember is that the basic **TRIM** principles still work, however you decide to implement them.

And what of the future? As Sam Goldwyn famously observed, you should never make forecasts, especially about the future – and this must be more true of the IT world than almost any other. What we can be certain of is that "computers" will get smaller and smaller, and more and more integrated into our lives. 25 years ago the iPhone – a computer, diary, timepiece and camera that can tell us where we are on the globe to within 20 metres and connect us to virtually all the knowledge in the world – would have seemed like impossible science fiction.

The way we communicate, remember things and even think is changing with ever-greater speed. It seems inevitable that the iPhone, with even greater powers, will eventually move from our pocket into our head....

Maybe by that stage there will be no need for **TRIM** training – those who want to will just download a tiny **TRIM** app into their brain, and most of their problems will be solved! But no machine is ever going to be able to choose our North Pole Goal for us – or, I suspect, work out the best way to achieve it! We will always strive to retain our own freedom of choice – and that means the ability to make mistakes. We'll always want to ensure that we are valued and liked by people close to us. We'll always need **TRIM**, in one form or another!

Tricks, Traps and Temptations

10th Dan **TRIM**!

> Experience
> is the
> teacher of
> all things
>
> JULIUS CAESAR

As you know **TRIM** always leaves you with plenty of options for customising the way you organise life. Everyone has their own way of doing things and you will only get the best out of The **TRIM** Course Book if you are entirely happy with your own setup.

But having said that, there are lots of little tricks that will help you to tune-up your **TRIM** tools – and some traps and temptations that often cause problems. This chapter comes mainly from my own experience of teaching and living by **TRIM** for the past forty years – and from the experiences of my students in putting **TRIM** into practice!

TRICKS

TRAPS

TEMPTATIONS

TRICKS

Breaking Habits

Most of us are creatures of habit. We like our routines and feel most at ease well within our comfort zones: indeed, for much of the time we are so set in our ways that we operate on autopilot. This can make it difficult to remember to do things that involve a break in our routines.

For example, in an idle moment at work you might suddenly remember that you have run out of teabags at home (most of us occasionally have these flashes, usually completely unconnected with what we're doing at the time!) Buying teabags isn't complicated: it just means stopping off at the shop on the way home.

But you drive past the shop every time you go to or from work. You could do it with your eyes closed. In fact, you could probably drive all the way to or from your house without ever actually thinking about what you are doing. It's more than just a habit – it's virtually a way of life.

So how are you going to stop yourself sailing past the shop this evening, and remember to buy the teabags? Sure, you will put a note in the appropriate part of your Terrain Map – but will that be enough to make you stop the car when the time comes....?

What you have to do is break your habit. You need something to remind you, at the right moment, to do something unusual.

In this situation I use a couple of techniques. The best, tried and tested, is to put down markers – literally. A Post-it note threaded onto the car keyring as soon as the action has popped into my head – then transferred to the steering wheel as I get into the car. The note winks at me as I drive home.

But will this be enough to jog my memory twenty minutes later, as I'm actually approaching the shop? I know that I'm quite capable of setting out with every good intention, but still forgetting to stop at the vital moment. Well, if I still don't stop for the teabags, I have only myself to blame for my unsatisfied urge for a cup of tea!

So my other technique is to use a form of Visualisation, or even Mental Rehearsal: I make a conscious effort to imagine myself walking into the shop, try to visualise exactly where the teabags are stored, and remember the shopkeeper's face. All of this helps to imprint the idea of stopping at the shop in my mind – and I can even make it into a kind of game, to see whether I have remembered correctly where to find the teabags, or imagined the right person behind the till.

Finally, of course, if you've got the toys you can resort to technology – set an alarm or reminder on your mobile phone, timed to go off a few minutes before you are due to drive past the shop. If you're supersophisticated (or perhaps just extremely sad....) you can use your iPhone and Siri to set an alarm to beep when it senses that you're in the right area.

One way or another, when you arrive home you will certainly have earned your cuppa!

Five minutes early

The world is pretty evenly divided into people who are five minutes early, and those who are five minutes late. You've probably noticed – at meetings, going to the cinema, getting together for a meal – that it's always the same people who turn up late.

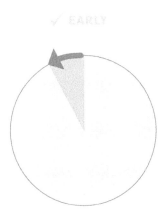

Although they often look flustered, and are full of apologies and excuses, there's a lingering feeling that being late demonstrates that they don't regard the people waiting for them as particularly important: "Yes, I'll agree to meet you then – but if I've got something more pressing to do, that's your bad luck and you'll just have to wait for me...." So they start off by giving a bad impression, and often then compound it because their embarrassment and fluster prevents them from performing as well as they could.

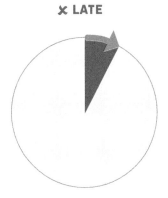

Oddly enough, the worst offenders are often the optimists. Deep down, they believe (and plan on the basis that) the bus really will arrive at the stop around the same time they do. For once, the train won't be 15 minutes late this time. They really have got time just to nip into the supermarket on the way to the meeting.

Don't do it! Arriving late for things really annoys the people who took the trouble to get there on time – and if you make a habit of it, they may well begin to resent it. The inconvenient truth is that almost always, if you are late it is because you chose to be late.

In this area, be a pessimist! If you work on the basis of Murphy's Law – that if things can go wrong, they probably will – then you can err on the safe side. Assume that a 30-minute journey will take 40 minutes; that there will inevitably be a broken-down car on the motorway; that the babysitter will not arrive on time. Always plan to arrive at least 5 minutes early, everywhere and for everything.

Of course, having arrived ahead of time doesn't mean that you should always announce yourself immediately! As everyone who has had friends round for dinner can confirm, there is nothing worse than the guest who arrives early – usually just as the final preparations are being completed. If you are going to a business meeting, take some work with you: if everything actually goes according to plan, and you do get there with that few minutes in hand, you can sit and do some reading or whatever till the time comes. This could even be the same work that you were tempted to finish off before you left – but didn't because it might make you late! If your appointment is social, you will have an extra few minutes to catch up with your friends – and enjoy the moral high ground while you wait for Alice, who is always blooming well late!

Here is a thought: if I was promised £1million for arriving on time would you like to bet against me being punctual? This is a good response to Alice when she blames "things" for making her late yet again!

JUST FOR ARRIVING ON TIME

The Royal Bank of £1,000,000
TRIM

ONE MILLION POUNDS
STERLING

£1,000,000

Watch your timings

It follows from the last point that you should always keep an eye on the time – and check your Terrain Map to see what you're supposed to be doing next, and where you need to be.

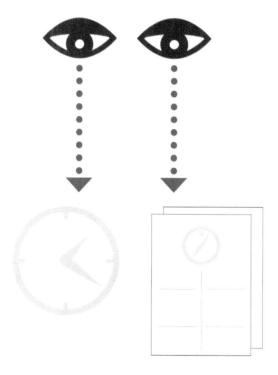

If you have finished one task, and have a few minutes before you are due to leave for the next one, there is always a temptation to try to fit something in before you go.

Resist it! Don't try to squeeze as much as possible out of the time available now if you risk messing up the start of the next thing you need to move onto. If you do, the chances are that you will make a poor job of what you're trying to shoehorn in, and also get off on the wrong foot for the new task.

Much better to look at your Terrain Map, and either find something that you are confident you really can do properly in the time available, or simply take some extra time to just sit and think!

Control your 'incoming fire'

Most of the time you have a reasonable degree of control over how you distribute your time – even if it's taken up with attending meetings arranged by other people, you know how much time you need to allocate, when you need to leave, how much time you should have before your next appointment, and so on.

So: you have fifteen minutes before an important meeting starts. You know it will take you ten minutes to get there – and, being a good **TRIM**-trained person, you want to arrive for the meeting five minutes early. You have all your papers ready – you should leave now.

The phone rings. Why answer it?

Stuart here.

Hello Stuart, it's John Brown from Great Big Company about our Events Day Out next month.

Sorry, John, I'm just heading off for a meeting, I'll give you a call later on today.

Oh – OK. Look forward to hearing from you. Enjoy your meeting...

What does John Brown take from this conversation?

- Stuart reckons that getting to his meeting on time is more important than speaking to John Brown
- Stuart hasn't got the common sense to put his phone on to 'voicemail'
- Stuart is either one of the last people in the world not to have a phone that shows him who's calling, or he can't resist picking up a call!

There really is no reason at all for answering a phone call if it risks making you late for an appointment. Letting it go to voicemail means that

- You get to your meeting in time to start off well
- Your caller doesn't get fobbed off and probably offended when you have to tell them that, right now, you have more important things to do than speak to them
- You can listen to their message and consider your response before you call them back
- You can impress them, and show how much you love them, by actually returning their call!

Of course there may be calls that you would always want to take, even if this meant being late for your meeting – from a senior boss, about a family emergency, or whatever. Your phone's caller display will probably at least tell you who is calling, if not what they are calling about – and if you are concerned, you can probably still steal a minute or two to listen to the voice message, so you can decide on your course of action before you have to leave. The message might even be about cancelling the meeting!

With this information you always have the opportunity to consider the actions available, and the costs and benefits of these actions.

Always have something to do

As all good **TRIM** Course graduates know, time is our most precious resource: we can't buy more of it, or store it to use later. So whatever else we do, we have to use our time wisely.

I've already pointed out that it really is important and stress-saving to plan to arrive everywhere five minutes ahead of time: you have a little slack if delays happen, you will turn up more relaxed and you'll perform better. But of course, usually the bus will be punctual and the motorway will be clear – so when you have arrived where you need to be, you will have a little spare time, all of your own. And when the person you are meeting calls to say that they have been delayed for 20 minutes, you will have quite a significant chunk of your day, suddenly freed up for you to use however you want to. Another small Gift of Time!

That's why it's worth always taking along something worthwhile to do. If you're on your way to a business meeting, you may choose to do a little extra Virtual Rehearsal before it starts – or just tackle a few bits that you've picked up from your reading pile. You may just want to catch up on news and emails on your phone – or even use it to make a few of the phone calls from your Terrain Map.

But let's not be too puritanical about this! The spare time you have is your own, to do with as you will – so if you want to spend it blasting a few aliens in your favourite game, or reading a magazine, or even just dreaming and listening to some music – go for it! Just remember to appreciate what you are doing, rather than just thinking of it as 'passing the time'.

Gift of time!

Batching jobs to do

If you have a load of phonecalls to make – try to do them one after the other, rather than fitting other things in between. You'll probably need to have the same items to hand – your **Diaries** and **Folders** – and you may well be talking about the same subject to different people.

This applies especially if you're making sales calls. Most people dislike cold-calling – both making and accepting the calls! But if you need to make them, you will find that if you do a number in sequence you will become more fluent and natural as the calls progress. Of course this only goes so far – you need to have a break, and do something different, when you feel yourself getting tired and stale.

Batching applies to all sorts of jobs, not just phone calls. Once you get into a rhythm of answering emails, writing letters or even just reading memos you will find that your speed and accuracy picks up as you go along.

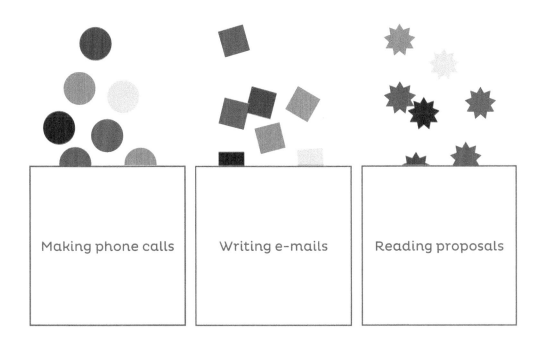

| Making phone calls | Writing e-mails | Reading proposals |

Filing

Dreadful word! Nobody likes filing. Filing is not a sensible occupation for a grown-up human being.

But we all need to do it – a bit, anyway. As you have seen throughout the **TRIM** Course book, you always need to have access to the right information at the right time, and in the right place. Well, you can't do that without making sure that you put it where it's supposed to be!

I have banged on throughout the book about the importance of posting information to '**Places to Be**' and '**Things to Do**' diaries, to **People Folders** and **Subject Folders**, and above all to Terrain Maps. It's true – all these information stores need to be carefully tended and kept up to date, otherwise they could become useless or even misleading.

So what's the answer? Nobody wants to spend an hour a day filing away bits of information – a little bit here, a little bit there (copied over here). In fact, in the real world of course nobody would actually do it! Yet thousands of people have benefited from the **TRIM** Course and use it every day. How do they manage it....?

Well, you have seen part of the answer in Chapter 10 on Digital **TRIM**. Our computers, mobiles and tablets have made a huge difference to the ease with which we can enter, store and retrieve information. You can put information into one application, and retrieve it in many different ways depending on how you need to use it.

But the main point is that as you become more familiar with the **TRIM** tools and techniques, you will also gain a much clearer idea of just what information is valuable, why, and where it needs to be stored. When you actually understand the reasons, and see for yourself the benefit of keeping appropriate information, it is much easier to select the right data to store and decide where to put it. In time it will become second nature.

What you must avoid at all costs is letting your information build up, so that you can 'really get down to it' and deal with it in one session – whether once a day, or once a week. Neither will work – and both will just make you unhappy! If you have to knuckle down to dealing with a whole day's worth of stuff, or even more, then you will certainly forget to put down some vital information – and you certainly won't enjoy the chore!

THE ONLY WAY TO KEEP EVERYTHING TICKING ALONG EFFICIENTLY WITHOUT EITHER LOSING INFORMATION OR BORING YOURSELF TO TEARS IS TO DO IT AS YOU GO ALONG.

Record data, update diaries, add to your contact information as soon as possible after the event you're dealing with. That way everything is fresh in your mind, it will take no time at all and it will be there when you next need it.

Emails

We all get far too many emails, and they fall roughly into three categories:

SPAM

In many ways the most annoying, but the easiest to deal with. For a start, use the best spam filter you can. Most ISPs offer one, and several applications also filter out rubbish. These should all be regularly and automatically updated to deal with whatever is the current wave of nonsense being sprayed out to millions of addresses every day – and with most, you are able to configure them to filter out specific senders who are being missed by the automated system.

When spam does get through to your inbox, it is rarely worthwhile bothering to 'unsubscribe' from it unless you know that the sender is genuine. Many illegal spammers are delighted to receive unsubscribe messages – it proves that the email address is genuine, and makes it more valuable for selling on.

GENUINE BUT UNIMPORTANT OR NON-URGENT

The vast majority of emails fall into this category. Try to separate them out in your email program's folders, into ones that need a response, or some action, and those that are worth keeping because they might be interesting to read later. The residue can be deleted straight away!

Then you can try using the 'two-minute rule' – if the mail needs action and this can be done in less than two minutes, do it and get rid of it! This also applies to non-essential emails – a courteous response is simply good manners, can normally be sent off very quickly, and will keep the sender onside! The small investment of your time might well pay off handsomely.

Set up a 'reading' folder on your email accounts into which you can put the emails that might be interesting to read later. If you can access this from your phone or tablet, it can provide the perfect way of spending any spare time you might have from arriving early for meetings!

IMPORTANT AND URGENT EMAILS

Note that I used both of the words 'important' and 'urgent' – remember what we said in Chapter 4, where we saw that everything important was not urgent, and vice versa. Some people still appear to believe that because they have sent something by email, it will automatically be treated as a matter of urgency and a reply will arrive within minutes. These days, when the great majority of business mail is sent electronically, this is emphatically not the case!

However, some emails certainly do need to be given the 'Top Priority' treatment, and in this case clearly you need to take action fast. Just remember to update your Terrain Map, adding tasks that have just popped up and reshuffling others when necessary.

ACTION
 < 2 minutes - deal with straight away
 > 2 minutes - file for actioning later
READING FOLDER
BIN

The 'Gift of Time'

What's a your reaction when someone calls at the last minute to say they can't make a meeting – or they need to cut it short by half an hour? Probably you feel a bit annoyed.

On the other hand, occasionally a supplier might unexpectedly produce your order a day earlier than they had estimated, or you might find that a journey takes an hour less time than you expected. In these cases you're probably quite happy!

In fact, these developments both represent a 'Gift of Time'. Without having to actually do anything, you find yourself with extra time available on your Terrain Map. So instead of being cross at the person who has let you down by missing a meeting, or just enjoying your luck at arriving early – use the gift you have been given!

You may remember that right at the start of this book I talked about the two things you always have to offer other people – your abilities, and your time. Time really is a valuable thing to have – especially if, like some working people today, your are 'money rich but time poor'. If you suddenly find you have more of it than you thought, make the most of it.

As we saw in the last section, it's worthwhile always having something on hand to do. I talked before about always arriving 5 minutes early: but of course the same principles apply if you suddenly receive a gift of time. Depending on how much becomes available, you might be able to tackle something on your Terrain Map – or even embark on something you had not expected to start for a while. Or you might just want to relax!

You can also pass on your gift. If you have undertaken to complete some work, or provide a service to someone by a specific time – maybe you can give them a pleasant surprise by finishing it earlier than you had promised. This will increase their trust in you and make them more willing to use your services next time.

However, do not be too early without warning them! After all your previous negotiating with them on the delivery time, if you then come in a lot earlier without any warning and explanation they may well rightly decide next time not to be so accommodating to you on timings for the next project you are asked to deliver for them. They might even decide that if you are so early you might not be quite as good as they had previously thought!

Worth a thought: When you offer a gift of time on a promise you have previously made, offer it around. Start with a few people who will reply "thanks for the offer, but I am okay with the original timings". Once you get to the person that says "that would be great" you have quite a few other people impressed with your generosity in offering them your gift of time.

It takes practise to make sure that the early offers are gratefully declined before the lucky recipient says "yes, thanks a lot"

Of course there may be a downside. If the gift of time you receive is because someone has failed to make it to a meeting, or a supplier has let you down, then you're probably going to have to reschedule. What you have received may be more 'a loan of time' than a gift! However, now you are firmly in control. You're in a strong position to ensure that the re-arranged meeting or delivery suits your timetable rather than the other person's – and you may even be able to negotiate a discount or better terms for the next time.

TRAPS

Not returning calls

Anyone who uses voicemail sensibly – as of course all good **TRIMMERS** do! – receives innumerable requests for calls back. Good callers will normally give you some idea of what they want to talk about, so that you can be prepared when you return their call. Bad callers will either give you no clue (always a warning sign!) or insist on leaving a three minute message giving you all the information they wanted to impart, but still demanding that you call them back to hear it all again.

The good callers are not a problem. You know what the subject is, how urgent it is to call back, and roughly how long the call is going to take. Even if you have no interest in what the caller wants to talk about, it makes sense to return the call – a call back is a worthwhile courtesy and avoids wasting both the caller's time and your own with a further voicemail message. And you never know when you might need the caller's services in future!

Inefficient message-leavers are more of a problem. Especially if their message gives you no clue as to what they want to talk about, the temptation is to ignore the voicemail and not return the call. There's a good chance that it's a sales call, with someone trying to sell you anything from insurance to new windows. Why should you spend time calling them back?

Well... it's worth looking at the potential costs and benefits. The apparent benefit is that not calling back saves you the time and effort of making the call – very tempting, especially if you know you're not interested in whatever is likely to be offered. However, the cost will probably be yet another voicemail, or even worse a call that you actually answer at a potentially inconvenient time. In other words, in the long run you are unlikely actually to save any time at all, and might give yourself more inconvenience than you avoid. And it's always possible that you might miss an offer you shouldn't refuse!

It's usually best just to knock the whole thing on the head with a quick, polite call back making it clear that you're not interested – it will probably take less than half a minute and you can to it at any time that's convenient for you. If you get the caller's own voicemail, your call can be shorter still!

The person who leaves an interminable message, but still wants you to call back, is even more of a nuisance: they have taken up your time giving you a load of information, but nevertheless want you to ring back to hear it all again! To be fair, some callers are able to leave a message which sets out a problem and simply asks you for a decision without going through all the arguments again – but they are regrettably rare!

I often respond to long voicemails with a short phone call thanking the person for their message and explaining that it contained so much useful information that I could consider it more easily if they sent me an email. This normally ensures that they are a bit more concise in presenting the message! It also allows me to give it more thought and respond in my own time.

Of course this approach is often not possible – the leavers of long messages are not usually business contacts, who tend to be a bit more efficient, but friends or relatives who might not have email anyway. In this case the best response is a pre-emptive strike: work out from their voicemail what decision they are trying to achieve, or what more information they would like to have, and start your call back from that point. "Thank you for your message, Aunt Hattie. I'm looking forward to seeing you and Uncle George when you arrive on the 7.30 train on Thursday after you've seen your lawyer. I will collect you from the station."

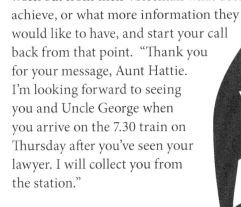

Out-of-office, out-of-date!

There are few more annoying messages than the ones which tell you that the caller is out of the office until Wednesday the 8th, when you are actually calling on Friday the 10th! This is as true of email out-of-office messages as it is of voicemails.

DO PEOPLE JUST FORGET, OR DO THEY SIMPLY NOT CARE?

I don't know – either way, it's a pretty clear demonstration that they are not on the ball.

Automated answering services

Unless you are a mega-company (or even if you are!) there's no excuse for having some Digital Dorothy reading callers their rights and then inviting them to drill down through three separate lists of options before they get to speak to a human being. It shows that you care more about your costs than your customers' satisfaction, and is a clear invitation to them to go somewhere else next time.

You may genuinely need to use voicemail a lot – if you spend most of your time teaching, or in meetings, or working in places where you can't use your mobile phone, or whatever.

In this case, it's especially important to get your greeting message right. Make sure that
→ you say who you are – people don't like leaving messages unless they are confident they have called the right number
→ your message isn't too long – don't make your callers hang on for ages listening to a sales pitch, or an irrelevant reason why you can't take the call
→ you remind callers to leave their name and number
→ you only make a commitment to call back if you really will do it
→ you give some idea of when you'll be able to call back – or provide an alternative number that people can call immediately

Many smaller companies, especially in the building trade, rely on mobile phones and voicemail almost exclusively for communicating with customers – and potential customers. Yet for some reason they are often appallingly bad at returning calls. There is no quicker way of losing business!

Calls answered by a switchboard or PA

How often have you got through and asked to speak to John Smith, then been interrogated about your name, company and business, before the PA discovers (to her huge surprise, presumably) that Mr Smith is 'not available'?

And how did you feel about Mr Smith afterwards? Were you likely to want to do business with him – or his company?

If you're going to get some gateway guardian to front for you, at least agree some message that is not guaranteed to make callers feel insulted. If the guardian says something like 'I think John has just left for a meeting, but I'll see if he is still there', then at least it's less obvious to the caller that Mr Smith has simply decided he has better things to do than talk to them!

Phone to text to email

Very often it's important to have a record of discussions – both as a reference for the future, and in case of a legal dispute. Banks and insurance companies routinely record phone conversations, as a safeguard against claims that they did not act on client instructions – but this is not usually possible for small companies or individuals. In fact it's illegal to record phone conversations unless both parties are aware that it is being done – and in any case wading through hours of recorded speech is a very inefficient way of accessing information.

So, if you need to have decisions or agreements recorded so that you can produce them later, you shouldn't make them over the phone – or if you do, you should request a written version immediately afterwards.

For similar reasons, text messages are unsatisfactory if you need to exchange important information that you might want to refer to later on. Of course a text is great for telling someone that you are running late, or which plane you're on. However, they are usually not kept for future reference, they are difficult to forward and they can't be printed or transferred to a computer.

EMAILS ARE ACCEPTED AS LEGALLY BINDING, AND CAN BE PRINTED, COPIED, FORWARDED AND ARCHIVED.

For anything formal, email is by far the best way of communicating. Almost everyone under the age of 70 – and many people well over it! – now has access to email, which is quick, cheap and can include attachments of pictures and scanned paper documents. Emails are accepted as legally binding, and can be printed, copied, forwarded and archived.

Probably the worst of all possible options is mixing the different media in one 'conversation', for instance by responding to an email with a text message. Occasionally it may be useful to discuss the content of an email on the phone, saving a great exchange of messages – but then it is essential to finish off with a further email recording the decisions made.

Shooting from the hip

It's often tempting to whizz off an instant response to an email, or pick up the phone straight away to answer a voicemail. For straightforward matters this may be exactly the right thing to do. If you are responding to anything more complicated – and especially if it's something on which you and the person you are replying to disagree – it's usually much better to wait a while, for three reasons:

→ the old advice to 'sleep on it' gives you time to mull over any problems – consciously or unconsciously – and will probably lead to a more effective reply
→ a hasty response may not cover all of the points you need to address – leading to a further round of messages leaving you back at square one. An e-mail in your in-box to deal with!
→ if the email was copied to others, delaying your own response may enable you to see how others have reacted and factor this in to your reply

So take a while longer and get your response right first time. Shooting from the hip may look good in cowboy movies, but it's not as effective as a well-aimed shot!

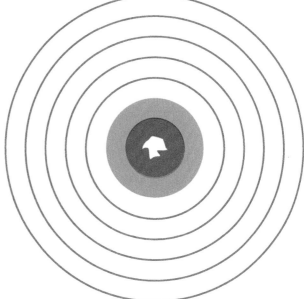

teabags !

Post-it Notes

Some people use Post-it notes, stuck on computer screens, desktops, chairs, bags and documents, instead of a To-Do list.

Don't do it! Post-its are a great invention for very short-term reminders, but they have many disadvantages:

→ they don't stick! The notes are carefully designed not to mark whatever they are posted on – but this means they are all too easy to dislodge and lose forever
→ they don't give any sense of priority or urgency to the tasks involved. Do you do the one at the top of your screen first, or the one at the bottom? Did you actually put the one at the top there yesterday morning? What about the one you have just found behind your desk?
→ they are difficult to update as situations develop and arrangements change

phone
John

Post-its are very good for one-off reminders, especially the ones that require you to change a long-standing routine – like the one on your car keys reminding you to interrupt your drive home to buy teabags. They are great for remembering what is inside an envelope, or marking references in a long document. But don't use them as a substitute To-Do list!

invoices

urgent!!

TEMPTATIONS

By this stage you have probably already adopted the **TRIM** tools and techniques, and adapted them to suit yourself. **TRIM** is not perfect, but I hope that by now you'll agree that it provides an excellent basis for living your life enjoyably, effectively and purposefully.

However, there are weaknesses in any such system – times when you know you should be doing things the right way, but it just seems like more trouble than it's worth. In this final section I'm going to look at some of the temptations you might face in using **TRIM** tools and techniques in real life situations.

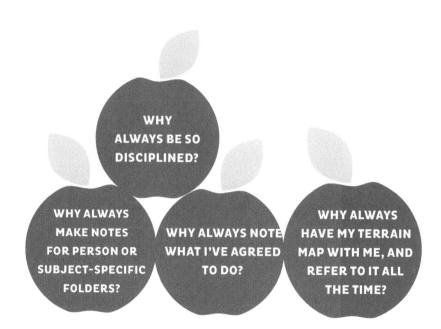

WHY ALWAYS BE SO DISCIPLINED?

WHY ALWAYS MAKE NOTES FOR PERSON OR SUBJECT-SPECIFIC FOLDERS?

WHY ALWAYS NOTE WHAT I'VE AGREED TO DO?

WHY ALWAYS HAVE MY TERRAIN MAP WITH ME, AND REFER TO IT ALL THE TIME?

Living dangerously

I can remember things!
Besides, it will be a fun challenge to kick over the traces and not be so efficient all of the time!

Let's live dangerously.

- → I've got the notes – but I'm not going to transfer them to their relevant places!
- → I'm in a meeting, talking to someone about a subject – but I'm not going to refer to the relevant folders!
- → I don't need to always refer to my Terrain Map – I'm going to be independent for once!

Yes, go for it – live dangerously once in a while. But I am confident that you will realise that you're getting it wrong far more often than you thought you would!

Remember why you started using the **TRIM** tools and techniques to begin with – to be efficient, and more importantly to be effective. To achieve your goals.

Remember your goals! Why deliberately underperform in trying to achieve them?

Illegible handwriting and cryptic notes

There's not much point in making notes if you can't both read and understand them afterwards. What a waste of effort!

- What was it you agreed to?
- When did you say you'd deliver it?
- What was it you wanted to do?
- What was that really important information you got?

Of course, you can take a guess – or just not bother trying to update your folders and diaries. But this will come back and bite you at some stage...

If you – even you! – can't read your writing, then you will either have to make a conscious effort to write more slowly or do a bit of practice. Oddly enough, writing is one area where practice really does pay off. Or perhaps you could try using a tablet computer, or even dictation software.

Cryptic notes are a great way of saving time if you can decrypt them later – but if you can't, they are just a waste of effort. If you often find you can't work out the meaning of what you wrote – don't complicate things in future.

Most of this really is down to practice. Almost no-one learns shorthand these days, but journalists are able to take notes for stories, and secretaries for the minutes of meetings and so on. Persevere – you will get better!

who?

JB bar4 ?

Losing paperwork

Don't! With a minimal amount of care, there's really no need to lose things. Make sure you backup all your digital stuff, and keep ephemeral items like Terrain Maps separate from your diaries. Try to post all your notes of interactions to the relevant places as soon as possible after the event.

Over-organising

Once you have read about the **TRIM** tools and techniques, you may be tempted to

→ Go back to square one and reorganise everything in your life before you can start using and benefiting from **TRIM**
→ Note everything, all of the time
→ Transfer everything to all of your folders
→ Refer to all your folders all the time

You don't need to do this! As with everything in life, it's a question of getting the balance right. Take things one at a time, in which ever order suits, at whatever speed suits you. Always remember that the objective of **TRIM** is to empower you and help you achieve your goals.

Over-organising can very easily be a subtle form of procrastination.

WHAT YOU NEED IS ACTION!

Shadow actions

It's easy to be seduced by the joy of crossing things off your Terrain Map. You become addicted to the need to complete tasks and score them out.

All good fun – but guard against the temptation to add contrived actions to your Terrain Map just for the satisfaction of crossing them off! Actions you add must help to achieve your goals – real and not contrived. As before, remember that the objective of **TRIM** is to empower you and help you achieve your goals.

YOUR NORTH POLE GOAL ⇨

THE SCHOOL OF TRIM

What next?

JFDI

INTERNET
ACRONYM

**CONGRATULATIONS – YOU HAVE
ALMOST FINISHED THE COURSE!**

This chapter summarises the main
elements of **TRIM** – and, I hope, gives
you a helpful push as you set off once
again on the slalom course of life!

HIGHLY
CONCENTRATED
ESSENCE OF TRIM

KEY 'MUST DOS'

THAT'S ALL FOLKS

THE WORLD WE LIVE IN

Time is limited and democratic. We all have only the same amount. We can't 'manage it' – we can only decide how we are going to use what we have

There are always more things to do than we have time for – and there always will be

You never 'don't have time' to do anything – you simply choose to do something else instead

DECIDING HOW TO USE OUR TIME

Goal setting underpins all our choices

We need to have a clear picture of what we want to achieve in life – a North Pole Goal, which will help to set the progressively shorter-term goals that we can use to decide how we actually spend our time right now

We know that we'll have to make compromises to deal with pressures imposed by family, friends and others – but we don't lose sight of our targets, and we keep moving towards them even though there may be detours on the way

WORKING TOWARDS OUR GOALS

To attain our goals we need always to be aware of

Where we are now

Where we are going

How we will get there

Our journey will also be defined by

What we have committed ourselves to do

by when

to what level of quality or performance

MAKING OUR WAY THROUGH THE MAZE OF COMPETING PRESSURES

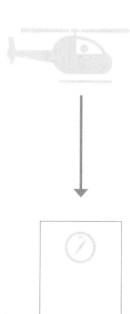

- We are continually involved in Interactions with others – face to face, by telephone, or electronically
- Our own brains also constantly bombard us with thoughts and ideas
- These interactions generate Actions – **Places to Be** and **Things to Do** – and Information – **People Specific** and **Subject Specific**
- The combination of Actions and Information leads to both 'quantity-driven' Efficiency and 'quality-driven' Effectiveness
- We need always to be able to capture the Actions and Information resulting from any Interaction, and to post them to the correct places as soon as possible after they arise

PLANNING AND MONITORING THE WAY WE ARE USING OUR TIME

- We need to have a regular weekly action to look forward and plan where we are going to be, and what we shall be doing, in the days ahead – the **Weekly Helicopter Trip**
- This forward planning needs to be transferred to a daily action sheet – the Terrain Map
- The Terrain Map tells you
  - where you are going today, and when you need to be there by
  - what you have to do along the way, and when it must be done by
- As Interactions happen throughout the day, you modify your Terrain Map accordingly to take account of changed circumstances and choices you make about how to use your time
- This is all about Efficiency – doing what you said you would do, never letting people down and never forgetting things you have committed to do

EFFICIENCY AND EFFECTIVENESS

- Efficiency is measured by quantity
- Effectiveness is measured by quality. How effective you are depends on how you use the two gifts that you have to offer others – your abilities and your time
- You can improve your abilities through experience and by training

THE FUNDAMENTALS OF TRIM

TRIM helps you to maximise your effectiveness, using the outcomes of Interactions – blended into your **Weekly Helicopter Trip** and Terrain Maps – to keep you moving towards your North Pole Goal.

NORTH POLE GOAL

247

KEY 'MUST DOS'

Only you can best decide how to use **TRIM**, by adapting the **TRIM** principles, tools and techniques to suit your own needs and preferences.

But although **TRIM** is very flexible, there are certain basic practices that I believe are essential.

PEN AND PAPER
Always be ready to make instant notes on the results of Interactions – and your own thoughts. Even if you normally use your phone or some other electronic device, keep a pen and paper available, if only for whenever you cannot gain access to the electronic device of your choice.

PUT INFORMATION IN THE RIGHT PLACE
If you can't put information in the right place straight away, transfer all your notes into relevant folders (or their electronic equivalents) as soon as possible.

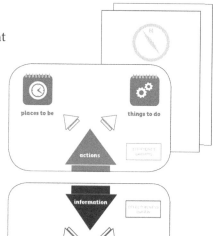

Actions – **Places to Be, Things to Do** – directly onto your Terrain Map for the appropriate day, otherwise into diaries/calendar. This is 'quantity driven' and leads to Efficiency

Information – **People Specific, Subject Specific** – into the right folders. This is 'quality driven' and leads to Effectiveness

REFER TO RELEVANT INFORMATION
Don't forget to refer to relevant folders and notes whenever dealing with a person or subject – preferably before, during and after!

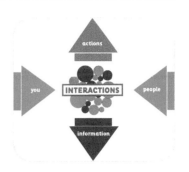

DEAL WITH INCOMING MATERIAL

Deal with all incoming material immediately – even if that's just a question of moving it to your 'action' folder

WEEKLY HELICOPTER TRIP

Make your **Weekly Helicopter Trip** a regular feature of your week – on the same day, and early enough to be before your day really gets going and you set off on your Terrain Map

WATCH YOUR WATCH!

Knowing the time locates you on your Terrain Map - where you should be now, how long you have before you need to be somewhere else, and what you should be doing.

FIVE MINUTES EARLY

Aim to be five minutes early to everything and everywhere.

BE IN THE MOMENT

Remember that what you are doing at any moment should be the most important thing to you at that time. Focus on it completely and don't be distracted.

TRANSFER ITEMS

Transfer items out of today's Terrain Map and re-assign them as soon as you know that more important things will prevent them from being done. Don't wait for the end of the day and depress yourself with all the things that you did not manage to do! In fact you can cheer yourself up by remembering that "The things left undone are just the price you pay for the things you have achieved!"

You now have a good understanding of all the **TRIM** tools and techniques, and as you use them you will manage your life more effectively and efficiently. Living by **TRIM** principles you will never make commitments that you can't fulfil, and never fail to fulfil a commitment. You will be trusted by your family, friends and colleagues and be at peace with yourself on your journey through life – well, at least for most of the time!

**I am confident that using your
newly-acquired abilities, you can be happy,
and make the world a better place!**

That's All Folks!

Congratulations!
You have successfully completed
The **TRIM** Course.

You now know that
TRIM requires discipline,
TRIM is hard work
...and **TRIM** works!

THE **TRIM** COURSE BOOK
RECOMMENDED READING

Napoleon Hill	Think and Grow Rich
Dale Carnegie	How to win friends and influence people
Stephen R. Covey	The 7 Habits of Highly Effective People
	The 8th Habit